Confident Kids

A Parent's Guide on How to Raise Confident

(The Ultimate Guide to Breaking the Cycle of Reactive Parenting)

Brandt Rohan

Published By **John Kembrey**

Brandt Rohan

All Rights Reserved

Confident Kids: A Parent's Guide on How to Raise Confident (The Ultimate Guide to Breaking the Cycle of Reactive Parenting)

ISBN 978-1-77485-887-5

No part of this guidebook shall be reproduced in any form without permission in writing from the publisher except in the case of brief quotations embodied in critical articles or reviews.

Legal & Disclaimer

The information contained in this ebook is not designed to replace or take the place of any form of medicine or professional medical advice. The information in this ebook has been provided for educational & entertainment purposes only.

The information contained in this book has been compiled from sources deemed reliable, and it is accurate to the best of the Author's knowledge; however, the Author cannot guarantee its accuracy and validity and cannot be held liable for any errors or omissions. Changes are periodically made to this book. You must consult your doctor or get professional medical advice before using any of the suggested remedies, techniques, or information in this book.

Upon using the information contained in this book, you agree to hold harmless the Author from and against any damages, costs, and expenses, including any legal fees potentially resulting from the application of any of the information provided by this guide. This disclaimer applies to any damages or injury caused by the use and application, whether directly or indirectly, of any advice or information presented, whether for breach of contract, tort, negligence, personal injury, criminal intent, or under any other cause of action.

You agree to accept all risks of using the information presented inside this book. You need to consult a professional medical practitioner in order to ensure you are both able and healthy enough to participate in this program.

TABLE OF CONTENTS

Chapter 1: It Starts In Your Mind (Mind In Mind Parenting) 1

Chapter 2: Raising Confident And Caring Children 14

Chapter 3: Managing Issues With Mindfulness 54

Chapter 4: Helping To Maintain Your Tranquil Home And Linking It All. 64

Chapter 5: Understanding About Parenting 73

Chapter 6: Ten Parenting Strategies You Should Know For Your Child (Boys And Girls) 97

Chapter 7: Speak The Right Things To Your Children 114

Chapter 8: Supporting Your Kids 147

Conclusion 184

Chapter 1: It Starts In Your Mind (Mind In Mind Parenting)

Mind-based parenting is a way of parenting that is tolerant of the unique emotions and thoughts of children. Parents believe that their children's behavior is important, and they tune to their children's needs about their needs, wants, and preferences. They are able to recognize their children's language and talk to children about the world of their minds.

This technique is linked to huge positive developmental outcomes, including the creation of secure attachment bonds, more interpersonal skills and perhaps more self-control.

Is it ever too late to begin? Is it too early to begin treating the child as a partner in conversation and seek meaning in what he says and does?

Psychologists Elizabeth Meins and Charles Fernyhough do not agree. There's a reason to believe that this approach is especially beneficial during the baby's first year.

Children thrive when their parents believe that they have their own thoughts and spend the time to discover what their babies are thinking and thinking and. In particular, infants are more likely to benefit from having "mind-minded" parental figures who can communicate effectively about their emotional and mental states.

Parents who are not careful are the ones who make comments that Meins and Fernyhough refer to as "appropriate remarks that are mind-focused," and the appropriateness of their comments is key.

I can see you're bored of the toy, as moms might be able to say.

Is this a normal conversation that is mind-focused? It is contingent on whether the child is bored. If he's showing signs of curiosity , such as looking at an object or or reaching for it, or grabbing it - then the comment isn't suitable. In order to be able to provide a mindful parenting approach caregivers should not just talk about feelings and concepts. They should provide statements that are pertinent to the situation at hand.

It's an important distinction as the mind-focused, good language that is spoken early in life can predict various development outcomes. Here's the facts.

Research suggests that mindful parenting can help babies establish solid bonds

It may seem absurd to view a baby's chatter as a serious form of dialogue.

However, in 1998 Elizabeth Meins noticed something she observed: Mothers who did this - mothers who were inclined to attribute importance to their children's first vocalisations -was most likely to be children who opened an entirely new space and were firmly bonded.

In different research, Meins and her colleagues observed babies as young as 6 months old playing with their mothers and collected instances of mind-related, spontaneous language. Researchers were particularly focused on acceptable comments, i.e., mother words that showed a clear understanding of what a baby was feeling.

Six months later, researchers looked at the infants their attachment bonds and found an obvious connection between attachment and parenting. Mothers who spoke more frequently suitable and appropriate remarks at the age of 6 months were more likely to have infants who were secure after 12 months.

Another study has shown that the early actions of mind-sets can determine the security of an attachment. Mind-oriented remarks that are in line with the norm are associated with secure connections with dads as with moms. They also have been associated to stable connections to childcare services.

When researchers from the Netherlands assessed three-year-olds who attended daycare centers, they discovered they were likely be deeply connected to their caregiver if she or she frequently made thoughts-focused remarks.

The evidence suggests that mind-focused parenting can help babies develop social skills

Apart from having strong connections, children who have mind-focused parents are also more likely demonstrate sophisticated thinking about the mental state of others. This is what psychologists refer to as "theory of the mind" capabilities. How can researchers assess this?

A key test is the test of false belief that requires children to discern between what is genuine and what an other (mistaken) person thinks to be the truth. Take the false belief test, which was developed by Meins and Fernyhough (1999). (1999). (1999). They urged children aged 5 to watch the puppet show and respond to specific questions.

The show started by having Charlie the Crocodile alone on the stage. He took a milk bottle and filled it up by popping soda.

Then Penny was the Penguin was seen emerging. She wasn't there to observe the actions of Charlie.

The researchers explained to the kids that Penny liked milk but rather than soda. They then asked the students to imagine the way Penny might be feeling when she looked at the milk glass. Do you think Penny be sad or happy?

The researchers then asked the students to guess what Penny might feel if she learned the truth. What would Penny feel when she looked into the carton to discover it was filled with soda and milk, but not soda inside?

Certain preschoolers could accurately predict what Penny's thinking (i.e. Penny would initially be delighted but then be disappointed later) These toddlers would be more likely receive pertinent, mind-focused compliments as they grew older.

The results have been replicated in subsequent research. In another study, the researchers observed moms interact with their 12-month-old infantsand observed the frequency at which parents used acceptable mind-based statements. They then investigated the theories of mind-based skills when toddlers reached the age of 4. A proper mind-minded conversation at the age of 12 months could predict children's ability to master the challenge of false beliefs at the age of 4.

In a study similar to this the researchers found that a correct brain-focused conversations in the infant years predicted, at the age of 51 months of age, the child's emotional comprehension as well as his or her performance in a test of false beliefs.

Another study suggests that the mother's early usage of appropriate, mind-focused words can help predict the child's ability to perceive perspectives throughout preschool and primary school years.

Does the conversation is important? Or is it the way you talk? Rory Devine and Clair Hughes have studied this issue during a recent study into the mind theory development.

The study followed 117 children as well as their families for 13 month. They examined both "parental mental conversations" as well as "parents inclined to see kids as agents in the mind". They also assessed children's understanding of the wrong notions.

What parenting behavior is more influential on the outcomes of children? It turns out that just talking -- speaking about feelings and thoughtssuggested a higher level of understanding of the mind's abilities.

What is the causation?

The research studies are based on correlations. They do not allow us to conclude that mind-centered parenting helps kids to develop stronger bonds or to develop a more advanced theory of mind abilities.

These results could indicate the existence of particular genes parents share with their children biologically and that favor the growth of all three of these things: mind-mindfulness attachment security, attachment security and early children's mind-reading.

In that case, mind-mindfulness may not be as much the reason for the stability of attachment and the early success of the task of false belief. It's a shared cause.

There is some evidence that supports this.

In the research studies on children's daycare, the preschoolers did not have genetic ties to their caregivers. However, the connection between mind-based expressions and secure attachmentwas not changed.

In a second investigationusing the tools of behavioural geneticsfound that hereditary factors have a minimal impact on the evolution of theory of mind-skills (Hughes and colleagues, 2005). (Hughes et al 2005). (Hughes et al 2005).

Additionally, a variety of research provide evidence for adolescents developing their mental perspective through exposure to discourse in the mind.

For instance, when experts have examined the growth of children who have siblings, they've found one interesting pattern: Having an older sibling helps in the formation of the mind's theory. The younger sibling isn't. We'd expect this that children will learn from the mentalistic languages of older, more socially savvy people while playing.

The evidence from cross-cultural perspectives is fascinating.

In the world where discussion of mental states is prohibited children exhibit huge gap in their understanding of theories of mind. They will eventually get there however it could require many years.

Researchers have conducted some sort of randomised controlled study of the issue. After collecting baseline assessment of the performance of tasks that require false beliefs specifically for children 3 years old and older, Heidemarie Lohman and Michael

Tomasello divided the children into two groups.

The children in both groups talked with an adult, who demonstrated a variety of unique objects that appeared to be deceitful like pen that had the form of the petals of a flower. However, the conversation was not as clear.

In one class, the adults spoke to the children about the bogus nature of the products by using terms such as "think" or "know." In this instance an adult could ask "What are you thinking this could be? ... It seemed like it was a flower. ...."

For the other group adults discussed the objects, but they didn't use to mental states. ("What's this? ?...

It's an blossom...

You can also write with it ...")

After the sessions, researchers revisited the children's comprehension of faulty ideas. The children who were educated with mental state language scored higher on the test of false belief. They also showed greater awareness of the differences between appearance and the reality.

Other benefits: Can mind-focused parenting teach children control?

It may at first seem like a big leap. However, research has shown that children who have a strong bond tend to have better self-regulation capabilities. They are more adept at managing their desires, internalizing standards and delaying pleasure.

It's also easy to understand the way that mind theory capabilities can help with control of one's self. The ability to recognize the thoughts of others helps toddlers identify their intentions and predict behavior. This helps toddlers to see that their self-control efforts can be recognized.

Learning the language of mental states is crucial to self-control. Children learn to stay on the right track through talking to themselves through their mouths or internal.

Mind-focused parenting can help promote self-control by fostering the concept of safety and mind. It may also help by teaching children the language they can use to control their moods and emotions.

Are there studies that support of these theories? The issue of mind-mindness and self-control isn't as extensively studied. However, the research that is available can be beneficial.

For instance in a study that followed Canadian kids, researchers discovered that a mind-focused parenting style from the beginning of early childhood predicted better self-regulation in toddlers aged 18 months.

In a recent study of Chinese children showed that mind-focused parenting during the first 9 months of life predicted greater self-control in children aged three years old.

For instance, they were more adept at controlling their emotions and were more likely to to delay pleasure if doing so would allow them to get a better reward for the near future.

However, other variables such as parents' education level and income levels not predicative. Also, maternal sensitivity was not a factor. the need to respond quickly to the baby's physical and emotional needs.

The research concludes that mind-centered parenting -- which involves the rightly adjusted mental dialogueis beyond "simply sensing" the needs of a child "and giving them material assistance." It could help children develop self-control.

Mind-focused parenting: What can you learn from it?

Certain of the behavioral differences observed in families is due to genetic differences. The genetic makeup of our DNA can cause us to be more or less susceptible to acquire different abilities.

However, there is evidence that parental care and support are essential and is particularly important for secure attachments and theories of mind abilities.

Mind-centered parenting -- focusing on and making thoughtful comments on mental state strengthens social connections and helps children comprehend the thoughts and emotions of others. Additionally there are reasons to suggest that mindful parenting could help children gain more self-control.

Chapter 2: Raising Confident And Caring Children

How to Build Confidence in Your Child:
Self-confidence is the key to the future of good mental well-being and social pleasure. It's the foundation of being a healthy child and is the pathway to success in adulthood. In all ages, how you feel about yourself can affect your behavior. Imagine a time that you felt particularly positive about yourself. It was probably easier to interact with other people and feel great about yourself. Use these tips and tricks to help you build confidence in your youngster.

The kid examines his reflection and likes the face who he sees. He ruminates on himself and is at ease with the person he perceives. He has to think of himself as the one who is able to achieve things and is worthy of love. Parents are the primary factor in a child's perception of self-worth.

Unsatisfactory Self-Image A lot of times, this causes behavior Troubles

Most of the problems with behavior that I come across for counselling result from a lack of self-esteem for parents and children. Why is one person pleasure to be around but another person always is a drag? Health-coach-MB The way people treat themselves, interact with others, do well at school, excel at work, and engage with their spouses all depend on their self-image.

Healthy Self-Worth does not mean that you're Arcissistic or arrogant.

If you have confident children who grow to be a healthy person that means that they have a clear understanding of their strengths and weaknesses while recognizing the positives and not focusing on the areas that need improvement. Because there is an evident connection between the way your child views himself and the way in which he behaves and behaves, it is vital to establish a discipline system to create an ego-focused child. In the early years the child is exposed to both positive effects (builders) and negative influences (breakers) (breakers). Parents can expose their children to builders, and help him in working through the breakers.

Tips to create a confident child

1. Practice Attachment Parenting

Imagine yourself as the parent of a baby that spends hours in the arms of a parent and is swaddled in a sling and breastfeeds at the right time while her crying is lovingly acknowledged. What is the way you imagine this baby is feeling?

The child is loved and the baby feels valued. Have you ever had a day, where you were greeted with many strokes and were showering with praise? It is likely that you felt very appreciated and loved. The child who is the victim of this type of high-touch parenting builds self-esteem. She feels good about what she does.

The ability to respond is the foundation of a child's self-worth. Baby's cues to be soothed, for instance, crying and needs to be fed or comforted. The caregiver responds quickly and consistently. Since this response-cue pattern repeats itself hundreds, perhaps thousands of times during the course of a year, the child realizes that the signals she gives her have significance: "Someone listens to me. So, I'm worth it."

Naturally, you cannot always respond quickly or in a consistent manner. It's the pattern that counts. There will be times where you're lacking patience. Children pick up the predominant parenting style and form impressions. As a baby grows older, it is crucial for him to be able to handle healthy irritation since this can help the child to adapt to changes. The most important thing is that you're there for him. That's the foundation on which newborns build their identity.

The confidence-building benefits that result from the reward of attachment-parenting, particularly when it comes to babies who have high needs. Because of their more urgent needs they're at a greater susceptible to receiving negative reactions. As attachment parenting develops the sensitivity of parents who are linked and infants with high needs and their parents, they begin to see their own self-esteem.

Through responsive care A connected child is aware of what to expect. In contrast the child who is not connected is confused. If his needs aren't satisfied , and his signals are not being met, he thinks that the signals aren't worthy of being delivered. It is then concluded that "I'm not worth it. I'm at the mercy others and there's absolutely nothing that I could do to help them."

We stress that the significance of early nurture because, during the first two years of life, the infant's brain is growing rapidly. This is the time that a newborn develops patterns of association - mental models of how things work. The brain of the developing infant is like a drawer for filing. Every file has a mental image of a message she provides as well as the answer she expects. After making a contact, the infant stores the mental image of the event. For instance, a child opens her arms, and a parent responds by lifting her arms. The repetition of these actions reinforces the patterns in the baby's memory and eventually, the emotions either good or sad are entwined to them. A drawer of files filled with mostly pleasant experiences and photos can trigger an impression in "rightness." Her sense of "well-being" will become an integral part of the infant's self-image.

Attachment Parenting gives the feeling Of "Well-Being":

Children who are accustomed to the sense of happiness through attachment parenting will spend the remainder of their lives trying to keep this feeling. Since they have a lot of knowledge about feeling happy and content, they are able to reestablish that normal feeling after a brief interruption. They are able to deal through life's adversities since they're driven to improve their sense of happiness and have incorporated it in their self-image. They can fall many times and fall a lot, but they're more likely to get in good shape. This is particularly true to a child who is at a disadvantage or appears to be coming to the world with a gap in their natural talents. Children who do not feel this sense of well-being from birth are unable to locate it, yet they don't know the things they're looking for since they don't understand what it feels like. This is why some infants who are able to experience attachment parenting during the beginning years are able to thrive despite having a difficult childhood due to family problems.

Take the case in the case of Baby Jessica, the two-year-old who, as a result of an infraction to the law was taken away from the warm and welcoming house of the adoptive family, whom were her parents since birth, and then handed to her parents from birth who were not familiar with her. She's likely to thrive as she found herself in an unorthodox setting with a sense of wellbeing that was cultivated by early childhood care. She will live throughout her entire existence retaining that feeling despite the loss she suffered.

Catching up on the latest news:

What if I didn't adhere to all the attachment techniques of parenting, you might think? Don't get too harsh on yourself. Babies are resilient naturally it's not too late to begin the habits that can help create an ebullient youngster. Learning to get to know your child's personality and observing things from their perspective will assist him in developing confidence in his own self. This kind of care strengthens the foundations of self-esteem and also helps to repair the damage. However, the sooner the cement is poured on the body, the more smoothly it moves on , and the longer it is held.

2. Increase Your Self-confidence

Parenting can be beneficial. When you take care of your children, you often heal yourself. One mother with a highly-need child at our clinic told us, "My baby brings out the best and most awful of my." If you have problems in your family history that affect your parenting, work through these issues. Consult a psychiatrist when they're affecting your ability to stay in a calm state and be able to parent effectively.

Raise a Confident Child by Healing Your Past, build-self-confidence.

The self-esteem of a child is built and not passed down through the generations. Certain parenting behaviors and personality traits, like anger and fearfulness that are taught in every generation. The birth of a child gives you with the opportunity to become the parent you'd like to have were. If you're struggling with low self-confidence, particularly in the case that you believe it's as due to the way you were raised, make steps to recover yourself and break the cycle of family. This exercise can help build confidence in your child (therapists refer to this as "passing on the top, and ignoring the rest")

Note down exactly what that your parents have done to build your self-image.

Write down the specific ways that your parents harmed your self-image.

Then, commit to replicating the great practices of your parents, and avoid all the other things. If you are struggling to complete this task by yourself, seek help from a trained professional. Both your child and you will gain.

Don't be too hard to Your Parent's:

They must have done the best they could considering their circumstances and the norms that were in place at the time. I can remember having a grandma tell one of her daughters, "I was a nice mother to you. I followed exactly the plan the doctor gave me." The mother of the day believed that a large part of her problems stemmed due to the strict schedule she had to follow when she was just a newborn. She was determined how to interpret the signals her infant gave her. I advised her to not blame her mother as the norm for parenting in the moment was to adhere to the "experts" suggestions on how to raise children. However, the present mother is more at ease being the one who knows her child best.

Polish Your Mirror:

It's impossible to present a nice face every day however, a parent's frustration could be passed to the child. Your child's eyes are to reflect his thoughts. If you're anxious you aren't able to think about the joyous feelings. In the first years children's view of himself is so connected to the mother's image of her self that a kind of mutual self-worth construct is a reality. What image do your reflections reflect to your child? They will look through a fake face to the person who is unhappy underneath. John wrote in a fill-in-the-blanks tribute to his mother posted: "I appreciate being with my mom the most when she's smiling."

Children see your discontent about yourself as a sign of unhappiness with them. Even infants realize that they must please their parents. As children grow older, they could start to feel responsible for their parents' satisfaction. If you're not happy you are, then you're not good enough (or adequate) (or adequate). If you're having severe anxiety or depression, you should seek assistance to deal with these issues before they harm your child.

3. Make a Positive Reflection

The self-image of a child comes not just from the things that a child perceives about herself, but also from the way she perceives other people view her. This is especially true for young children who discover their own self-image by watching their parents' reactions. Do you project positive or negative thoughts on your children? Do you provide her with the idea of a confident child that she's a joy to be with? Do her ideas and desires are important to you? Do you feel that her behavior is pleasing to you? If you give your child praise, she is taught to feel good about herself. She also will trust you to inform her when her behavior isn't a good fit. This is a way to discipline her. "All I need to do is stare at the girl in a specific manner and she will stop causing trouble," claimed one mother.

The mother had bathed her child's self-awareness through positive thoughts, and the child became accustomed to the way he felt at the recipient of these slaps. If the mother displayed an image of negativity and the child didn't feel the emotional impact it caused. He changed his behavior quickly to restore his sense of happiness.

Be Realistic:

It is impossible to be full of joy all the time, but still be human. Your child should be aware that parents experience bad days as well. Children might be able to discern fake joy. Your empathy for him will increase his sensitivity towards you. One day, they could end up raising your self-confidence.

Reuniting Humpty-Dumpty:

If you have a confident child You spend the first years building your child's confidence and then you spend the latter years securing it. A lot of children with thin skin require protection from situations they feel are difficult to handle. I was assessing five-year-old Thomas for his physical exam at school. Thomas was a sensitive child who's mother had been aiding him in developing a solid sense of self-worth. We were having a philosophical discussion about the long-term advantages of attachment parenting. Thomas seemed to be bored. He started hanging from my scale, which is a costly scale that's integrated to at the very top of an exam table.

My first concern was about the safety of my table. For me, it was more at risk than Thomas which is why I declared, "Thomas, would you please stop hanging from this weights?" Just when Thomas was about to fall off due to my mistake his mother intervened to make an emergency rescue, "...because Thomas is so strong." She knows how to hide behind the child's back.

4. Help a child feel confident through Playing Together

You'll discover lots about your child and yourself during the course of playing. Playtime gives your child the messagethat "You are worthy of my time. You're a worthy human being." The idea is generally acknowledged that children learn through playing. It helps improve a child's behavior by empowering him with feelings that are meaningful and a sense of accomplishment. Instead of seeing playtime as a chore, use it to improve your child's behaviour.

Let your child begin the Game:

One of the most important learning concepts parents need to be aware of is that an activity that is initiated through confidence-building exercises of the child keeps the attention of the child longer than the one suggested by the adult who is playing. The more learning occurs when the child decides on what they want to do. The play of children can also increase self-worth: "Dad likes to do the things that I do!" Of course, you're probably wondering, "Oh no, not playing that block game yet!" or "We've read this story a dozen many times!" That's the anguish of being a parent. You'll get tired with The Cat in the Hat even before your toddler. If you're looking to add something new to the traditional play, you can add your own twists and turns when the story develops. Take a moment to discuss the story: "What would you do in the event that you were the Cat in the Hat arrived at our front door?" "Let's transform this block tower into an underground car park."

Help your child feel special

Help your child become more confident by paying attention to the child's interests during the time of play. If you are in the presence of your child but your mind is elsewhere your child will realize that you've lost focus and neither of you will benefit from your time spent together. Your child is deprived of the significance of your presence by deciding that she's not worth your time. You lose the opportunity to understand and appreciate your child, and to re-learn what it means to be a child.

I remember the great time that six-month-old John my cousin and me had as part of the "play circle." I placed his face before me along with my favourite games (mine along with his) in an arc around him using my legs. This kept him in the circle and provided support in the event that the child, who was a beginning sitting position, began to fall forward. John was the only one I could pay attention to. John felt loved and I did too. Making all those adorable baby sounds is fun.

Parents Need to Play:

As a person who was always busy I had a difficult time getting to a child's level and playing in a chaotic, seemingly insignificant play. There were plenty of "more important" things to do on my agenda. Once I realized the value we could gain for each other the time we spent together, it became important. Play was therapeutic for me. I needed to take a break from other things to concentrate on the essential child who was, in no way understanding it, guiding me to let go and relax.

Play has allowed me to understand John's personality as well as his abilities at each stage of his development. The child is able to show his parents who he is and the other way around in play. The whole relationship is greatly improved. Play puts us at the same level as our children, allowing parents to look deep behind the eye and enter the minds of their youngsters. Spend time observing the simple pleasures of playing.

Play is an investment:

Think about playing time as one of the best investments to help develop an enthused child. It's possible that you're "wasting time" stacking blocks , when it is possible to be "doing something else" instead. Many adults are worried about the possibility and need to make efforts to take a step back from their own adult agenda. Of of course, you don't need to spend all day playing and neither will your child ever want to (unless you are able to detect your opposition) (unless they sense your opposition). What may appear to be something that's not worth your time can mean a lot to your child.

The more you are enthusiastic when you do things with your child early and the more the interest your child will show in sharing experiences with you later on when he's older. As your child develops you could include him in your activities and work, as being with you is the greatest reward. Imagine this as if you are doing the most crucial task on earth--raising the human being.

5. Make sure to address your child's name

What's in the name? The self-conscious, the little or the big. I vividly recall my grandfather's words to me about the importance of remembering and using names of individuals. This is a valuable lesson. The last time I was a premed student competing against a bunch of marketing students to get the summer position of sales. When I got the job I was unsure what the reason was that I, while less skilled, was chosen. "Because you remembered and used name names for all the interviewers."

When you address your child's name particularly when accompanied with eyes and hands conveys an "you're unique" message.

Engaging in an interaction by mentioning the name of the person you are engaging with can open doors, reduces boundaries, and may even help soften the discipline of correction. Children begin to understand the way you present your name to the message you are sending and the behaviors you anticipate. The typical use of a child's first name or nickname only in conversational conversations, "Jimmy, I admire the work you're doing." They enlarge messages by using the entire name for more impact "James Michael Carter! Stop!" One youngster we've been told refers to his entire name in the context of the "mad name" because that's what the parents hear when they are furious with him.

Direct Communication:

We've found that children with confidence in their self-esteem are more likely to refer to their friends and parents by name or by title. They feel confident and can be more confident when they interact with other people. Our 2-year-old Lauren is running through my office, shouting: "Hi, Dad!" The use of "Dad" affected me more than a sluggish "Hi!" A school-age child who feels comfortable calling adults with a name will be more able to seek assistance when required.

6. Use the Carry-Over Principle

To build a confident youngster as she grows older encourage her talents. She's a pro at everything, whether an adorable two-year-old who creates fantastic imaginary picnics or as a ten-year-old who enjoys dancing. In the past we've come across an occurrence we call the carry-over principle. Having a positive experience with an activity can boost the self-esteem of a child and then it is transferred to other endeavors. Our son is an innate athlete, however he was not attracted to academics. Based on the concept of carry-over we encouraged his passion for athletics and assisted him to work on academics. His academic performance improved as his confidence in himself increased. Be aware of your child's unique talents and encourage her to build on them, and then see the whole person emerge.

7. Help Your Child Set the Stage to be Successful

Aiding your child to develop their abilities and acquire skills is a part of discipline. If you notice a skill that your child does not have, help him to develop it. Find a balance between pushing and protecting. Both are necessary. If you don't push your child to take on the challenge something new, his capabilities don't develop and you've lost a great confidence boost. If you do not protect your child from unrealistic expectations, his sense of accomplishment is shattered.

Beware of Value-by-Comparisons:

Children evaluate their worth based on how others perceive their worth. And in our measuring-and-testing world, children's skills--and consequently their value--are judged compared to others. The child could achieve a dazzling .400 for the Softball Team, yet she'll feel inferior if the other players are hitting .500. If you're trying to make your child confident ensure that your child knows that you cherish her for her personality rather than how she performs. Make sure to give her lots of eyes, a gentle touch and unrestricted attention. That is, offer yourself up no matter the way the game or test of achievement goes.

Don't think that your child will excel in music, sports, or academics because you've done it. The only thing that your child will excel at is simply being herself. You must let her be aware that your love for her is not based on the way you view her work. It's a tough job for a parent who might have been taught to perform in order to earn the sake of love and acceptance.

Give a Sense of Confidence by Giving them the Wall of Fame:

The Carter Family Museum of achievements Our walls feature Hayden's trophies for cheerleading and awards for horses, Erin's, John's Little League photographs, etc. Every child is talented at some thing. Learn about it, develop it, put it in a frame, and then display it to the world. If your home doesn't have the wall above, then your child has missed his chance at superstardom. If you've got a kid who's not athletic, consider the scouting. Through Boy Scouts and Girl

Scouts all are winners and everyone gets a lot of badges. As children walk by their displays, they can see in a single glance between five and 10 years of accomplishment. This can give people a boost even in the midst of times when self-esteem is declining.

8. Help Your Child Be Home-Smart Before they are Street Smart

At some point in your parenting journey you might come across the idea that a child's age should be exposed with different values, in order to let him decide his own values. It may sound great but it's not likely to be effective. It's like allowing a ship to go on a voyage without a captain or rudder. It's only by chance that the ship make it to its location. Children are too important to leave to chance.

Be sure to monitor your child's friends:

The child's self-concept and values are shaped by the people who are important to himsuch as family teachers, coaches and religious leaders, scout leaders, and even friends. Parents are responsible to eliminate those who harm the child's character and to encourage those that build it , resulting in a more confident child. Maintain a close eye on your child's relationships. Begin by letting your child select his peers and then supervise the interactions. When you've finished an activity, evaluate your child's mood. Is he happy or angry? Are the two children and their parents compatible? The combination of a passive child with a the ability to be a leader is right if the child who is stronger is able to push your child up rather than bringing him down.

Although some children naturally search for companions independently, at times it's beneficial to help your child's environment by intentionally giving him access to acceptable peers. Certain groups of children naturally get along very well. If the group your child is in isn't displaying the proper chemical balance, it's best to be involved. Through being a monitor parent, Martha was able to assist one of our kids who was being coerced to steal our money. The junior racketeer from the area was arrested after Martha was suspicious of conversations on the phone and was able to listen in at one point. Our beloved seven-year-old was over his head and happy to be a part of the conversation when we interacted.

Maintain a child-friendly home:

Your home should be inviting to your child's friends. Sure, there will be more mess to get rid of however, it's well worth it. Participating in the community assists you in guiding your child and gives you the chance to evaluate the manner in which your child interacts with others and also to gain a better understanding of the personality of your child. You can determine which social behaviors are appropriate and which ones require refinement. You'll be able to implement discipline-based interventions on the spot that you can do together with your child in one session or in group therapy, if you feel the entire group requires refocusing. The roots of a young child's self-concept stem from the parents and caregivers who are supportive.

At the age of six becoming more influential, peer influence becomes important. The more rooted the foundations of self-confidence that are nurtured at home and self-esteem, the better equipped children have the ability to interact with their friends in a way that enhances their self-esteem, instead of tearing it down. They are able to manage peers who are fun to play with as well as the ones who cause trouble. If children are attached parents in this way, they are able to deal with multiple situations (family and grandparents or preschool and the Sunday class) with different rules very effectively. To develop a healthy social life the child needs to be comfortable with themselves before being able to feel comfortable with other people.

Stay with Homebase:

In the course of natural development children are able to venture from the familiar and into the unfamiliar. She experiences new things exactly the same way as a baby who is attached learns to separate to her mommy. It is normal for a baby to go back time and time again to the comfort of her familiar (her home and family) but she is increasingly thrown through the abyss of the unfamiliar. A young person needs to have a solid to a base. Being shy doesn't mean that a child has a negative self-image. She just needs an extra dose of confidence, so that she can adhere to her own inner timeline when it comes to adapting to new situations and relationships.

Parents often ask if the amount of time spent at home bases is normal. Examine the situation over the entire year. If there is no change in the child's inclination to go out, it could be dangerous. However, if you notice an increasing tendency to leave and your child has a tendency to drift out, then it is just a careful social growth, which is typical of children who are sensitive who can form certain significant and long-lasting bonds, not just a few superficial ones.

9. Create a confident child by letting go of labels

"I'm asthmatic" Seven-year-old Greg proudly told me when I inquired about the reason he came in my office. Actually, Greg did have asthma however, the medical issue was much simpler to deal with than the emotional ramifications of the diagnosis. A few breaths of asthma bronchial dilator, and his wheeze was less severe however, his diagnosis remained. I privately told his mother, Greg's mom that I had two issues to discuss with every child who has chronic illnesses including the condition itself and the reactions of family members and children to the illness.

Every child wants to be unique and, when they discover it is glued to it as an emblem. "Asthmatic" was Greg's brand name and he would wear it frequently. The entire day was centered around the condition and his family was focused on this aspect of Greg rather than the whole person. Instead of feeling empathy Greg's siblings and brothers had grown tired of having to deal with Greg's asthma. They were unable to go on certain holidays because Greg would get tired. It turned into a family illness and everyone, except Greg was forced into roles they did not enjoy.

To remove Greg's name is to degrade Greg's self-esteem. We came to an agreement. I would manage Greg's asthma; his family would be thrilled with Greg and we all tried to give "the asthmatic" the healthier name to use.

10. Be aware of the influences that affect your child.

Schools could be detrimental to the child's mental health. To help develop confidence in your child, the the choice of school (if you're lucky enough to have one) must be thoroughly scrutinized. The child who is linked to the classroom with his classmates with different backgrounds and levels of connection will have certain expectations will not be met in the classroom. Children confront the challenges of joining a new social environment with distinctive behavior. If a child is with his caregivers and is armed with a positive self-image, he will not be disturbed by these different behavior. He could stick with his play style. In other cases, he could be angry, which can cause anxiety on his young personality. If self-confidence isn't strong enough A child may see bullying or violence as normal and consider these behaviours part of his life or let himself be victimized.

School Influences:

When you reach the age of six, your child enters primary school, the other adults are a part of her life. They are the ones who hang close enough to influence her behavior and influence her morals. In the past the most important people in the lives of children came mostly from the family unit, however nowadays, in a world of mobile people children are more likely to be surrounded by a wider number of peers and people who are significant. Parents today should be vigilant about who models the appropriate behavior to their children.

There is confusion among families of parents who are disciplinarians. There are two sides to the story. One side are parents who believe it is important for their children to learn about different values as they grow up to ensure they are more open-minded in the future. On the other hand, there are parents who wish to shield their children from external influences or ideas which might contradict their own beliefs. Their child is raised in a bubble. In between the 2 extremes, is the best way to build confidence in a young person.

Find Middle Ground:

Injecting a child in the melting pot of different values at an early age, prior to having any idea of what values she holds could result in children who are so confused that she doesn't have a conscience or a standing value system. Parents who are too protective could result in an unthinking child. for herself, making her open to criticism or critical that she is able to condemn anyone with different opinions. The middle of the spectrum are the parents who places the child on a solid value system , and then guides her as she explores different values.

The child, who has a solid value system from the beginning and is more able to weigh the values of her parents against other options and create a solid code of ethics. It might differ from what parents'. It could include a mix of the beliefs of parents with a bit of alternative ideas acquired from instructors or classmates. But the most important point is that the child has an established value system that he can use to operate. He isn't a leaf that is pushed down the river, which decides to take the path with the least resistance, reaches the limits and eventually flows into a huge ocean of doubt. A lot of children struggle, often throughout their lives, to find ideals that could be taught in the early years and in the beginning of childhood.

Be True to Your Values:

Parents should not be misled by the smug term "latent" that is attributed to middle-aged children. This isn't the moment to relax and be reckless. It is at this age the time your children develop their morals and learn your value system. This is the only time throughout their lives that they must, at the very least when they are in the beginning will recognize their parents' values system. As they grow older, children establish their own standards through interactions with their family members, classmates and teachers, as well as through their church/synagogue friendships. They discover a wider world by embracing a variety of perspectives and behavior.

While they chat (endlessly) as they watch and play in a range of situations, they are learning about the ways they choose to react and act. Doing your best to force your ideals upon an teen whose main goal in life is to find his own values is a challenge. The best way to pass your ideals across is to "walk your talk" by doing what you believe in.

11. Let Your Child Be Responsible

Children need work. One of the most effective ways to help kids develop confidence in themselves and internalize values is to help maintain the home environment of the family both inside and outside. Encourage confident children by allowing them to do household chores. This helps them feel more productive and focus their attention on the desired behavior and their teaching skills. Use these suggestions:

At around the age of two, toddlers can complete simple chores around the house. To keep a toddler's attention think about tasks that your child already has shown the interest. Our two-year-old daughter, Lauren has a love for napkins. So we assigned her the chore of placing napkins on every table. One of our patients informed us that: "I couldn't keep our three-year-old from his vacuum. Therefore, I assigned him the job of sweeping the living room. He was entertained, and I even got some work done from him." Between the ages of between two and four years old, children will begin to feel a sense of accountability to parents and to himself and also to his property. When he is able to develop an understanding of his responsibility towards these items, a sense of duty to society can be easily developed at the next phase of development.

Tasks for ages 3-6

When they reach the age of three at which point, children can learn to wash tubs and sinks (with an abrasive sponge, and small amount of cleaning solution) (using an abrasive and a small container of cleaner). Young youngsters enjoy scrubbing. Three's and Four's like to sort the laundry into light and dark. When they reach five, they could be washing dishes every evening. You can teach him what you would like to happen (for example, food waste put in the trash, dishes cleaned and put in the dishwasher) (for example, putting excess food waste in trash, and dishes washed and then placed in the dishwasher). Be sure to use non-breakable plates and cups, and then place dishes that are dirty in the oven for cleaning at a later time with the help of an adult.

Tasks for 7+ years old:

At the age of seven, children will be cooking the food at least once each week, from start to finish. Help him make his favorite food, and then let him know how to select the things at the grocery store. Encourage children in school to cook their own lunches. Apart from giving children an understanding of the responsibility they have for their diet, they're more likely to eat the food they prepare. When they are instructed, the kid can be left to it in the kitchen with no mother hovering. Enjoy a chat and relax with your companion.

Help a child feel confident by offering special jobs:

Make a task "special," and it's more likely to be completed. Whatever meaning the word "special" is will surely bring about outcomes. Perhaps a youngster infers that "I must be exceptional since I receive a special job." A four-to-five-year-old can have pre-assigned duties, with reminders, of course. In order to establish order in our busy home and to signal: "It's tidy time." Make sure you have a designated space for each child to clean up. Children of all ages suffer some degree of job inertia especially when their chores become tedious and they lose their enthusiasm. Sometimes, however, kids have to be taught that work is more important than playing. To start by working with them, you can help them.

Design Job Maps

You can make this an activity to have a family reunion. Make a list of the chores that must be completed and let the children choose and rotate as they wish. The work is divided between paid jobs, those that which they earn money from but also non-paying ones which are a natural requirement of our children to enjoy the privilege of being part of our family. Expect to pay a larger amount of money on unpopular tasks. It is best to pay the bill as soon as the job is completed because children are primarily focused on immediate rewards. At the next stage of development, between five to ten, young children might begin to realize to the fact that more privileges mean greater responsibility. When we made the decision to purchase a cottage for the family we envisioned to make Saturday mornings a family-focused fix-up time at the cottage and only when the task was completed would the fun commence.

Create a Family Garden:

Gardening can teach children to reap the fruits of what they plant. In our time as a family, we spent time in the garden in the early years, when our kids were younger, we joined in the maintenance of a garden and tending to the plants: Water them and they will grow as well as keep the weeds at bay and the flowers will bloom more effectively. Other chores that children and teenagers love and enjoy when taught by a parent include washing the car and cleaning the outside areas of living and walkways and gardens cleaning, vacuuming, dusting and baby-care. When they reach seven or eight years old, children are able to throw on loads of clothes and by the time they reach 10, they'll be doing their laundry.

If children are required to perform duties around the home Parents are not just let off their responsibilities Children also feel like they're helping the cause. They feel valued and appreciated. They feel valued and appreciated. on the home becomes an investment in the property's value.

12. Encourage children to let their feelings be expressed and not just stuff, their Thoughts

Develop confident children by teaching them to express their emotions easily. Being able to express emotions easily doesn't mean that the child is allowed to explode at every emotion anxiety, but rather, they find an acceptable balance between expressing and managing emotions. The goal is to control her emotions when necessary however not in a way that she's unable to open the lid within the context of a "safe" situation for example, like exercise (i.e. running around like wild to let off the steam) or in the company of an amiable companion.

All babies freely share their thoughts. The maturation process is a result of learning to remain cool in stressful situations. Young people who are uncontrolled in their emotions is brat. Someone who isn't able to express emotions becomes too restrained. A lack of control as well as too much emotional expression could cause problems in adulthood. The act of suffocating sentiments does no harm to the children, parents, or for the relationship. It tells the child that you're in danger because of her feelings or she gets the impression that you don't want to be able to understand her feelings.

Responsive Parents:

The child takes on your behavior and discovers that having or expressing emotions isn't appropriate. The youngster is convinced that the emotions that come with the ups and the downs of life do not have any value. A child's thinking is that when her feelings aren't significant, then she's not worthy. If the unfeeling loop is repeated time and time again and over again, the child will soon be taught to shut down the emotions and, more importantly, to conceal the feelings from her parents.

More destructive than being indifferent is when parents respond to children's emotions with angry messages, "I don't want to hear another yelling at the stupid shark!" The anxiety of parents reacting to their child's feelings makes a child an emotional suffocator.

The bright side is that you can think about what happens when a child feels comfortable to express her feelings, and a parent backs the sentiments of her child. Think about this scenario: "Daddy, the jewellery Grandma bought to me as a present for my birthday was damaged." Dad stops whatever is going on and focuses at his daughter, gazing into her eyes before placing his hands on her shoulder. He states, "I'm sorry. That's a gorgeous necklace." His words and body language convey: "I am open to your feelings; they count for me. I value you." The reply allows the youngster to share the truth about what she is feeling and deal with them by speaking to him. Instead of escaping into her shell or bursting into an angry rage, she has had the opportunity to voice her frustration. He has also boosted her self-worth by acknowledging and recognizing her feelings as a reflection of her.

Do You owe your child self-esteem?

Parents can misunderstand the concept of self-esteem and believe that this is just one more thing they must provide their child, along with regular meals as well as a warm winter coat. They will fight anything that can weaken self-esteemto the point where it's absurd. ("Oh, Billy, you aren't singing with a flat voice. It's just that you're challenging your tone.") The singers evaluate self-esteem on a daily basis, just as they would take an temperature. ("Julie's self-esteem is not great today. Her brother beat her at the checkers game the other night.") Each infant who is taken care of have self-esteem inbuilt. Much like an arborist who cares for trees, to raise an confident child, you need to take care of what's already there, and take every step to organize your child's environment so that she can grow sturdy and straight. Also, avoid cutting away the delicate branches.

You shouldn't build your child's self-esteem with a compliment or compliment, or activity by activity. Parents are already stricken with guilt due to the fact that they may not have done enough to increase their child's self-esteem. There is no need for a master's diploma in psychology to help raise an confident child. The majority of parenting is simple and relaxing. You can hold your child a lot and respond with kindness to the demands of her, and love your child. Relax and admire the person whose self-esteem is rising rapidly.

Chapter 3: Managing Issues With Mindfulness

Mindful parenting occurs when you pay focus to the situation instead of being distracted by your feelings.

What is your stress like?

Our brains and bodies are programmed to respond to stress-related situations in order to provide an emergency safety net. If our brain detects an imminent threat, it triggers the amygdala which is the brain's "alarm" system that will prompt our body to act without thinking. The amygdala is able to respond to events by triggering an instinctive fight or flight or freeze response. This is in order to safeguard us, however the stress receptors can't distinguish between genuine dangers and fake dangers. As parents the stress response frequently is activated in a way that is inappropriately triggered by events which aren't life-threatening. Our bodies react to our child spilling cereal all across the floor, the same way that we would react if being chased by bears.

Based on the events of your childhood and memories Your stress response could be more intense than someone else's. When our stress receptors are activated and we are unable to think clearly and paying attention to the people around us. We're not able to control our responses and are unable to staying focused, and our ability to resolve issues is reduced.

The Dr. Dan Siegel, a psychologist in the field of clinical psychology who studies the brain, says that in times of difficult parenting, it is possible to "lose the control" and "flip our lids" and let our emotions to guide our actions. If you "fly off the handle" it happens so quickly and we don't think about how our children view us. Our actions can be uncomfortable for children. Additionally, we're modeling the way grown-ups respond to pressure. If we decide to be more mindful by waiting to respond, then we could teach children that they, also, have the ability to pause, and decide to take action rather than react.

What does mindfulness mean in the context of parenting?

Controlling our emotional and physical actions is the first step in teaching children how to manage their emotions. That's why airlines tell us to put on our oxygen masks on prior to being able to put on the masks of our children. You have to be controlled before you can set the example of regulation to your children. If you're exhausted, stressed and stressed you won't be able to provide the necessary support the child you love.

Mindful parenting doesn't mean being an "perfect parenting expert" and isn't something that you are able to fail at. It's not easy, and it requires practice but as with all areas of parenting, there are days that are fantastic and others terrible, and you are able to take a second look. You might forget to stay alert, but if you realize you're distracted, you have an opportunity to take an alternative decision, the choice to remain present.

Mindful parenting means that you pay attention to what's happening rather than being swept away by your feelings. Mindfulness is about being free of shame and guilt over the past, and focusing on the present moment. It's about accepting whatever is taking place, not trying to change it or to ignore it.

The term "mindful parent" requires that you are aware of the situation you're in. This does not mean that you don't feel upset or angry. Of course, you'll have strong emotional states, yet acting upon the emotions blindly is what ruins our parenting.

The benefits of mindful parenting

You are aware of your thoughts and feelings.

You are more aware and attentive to your child's ideas, needs and thoughts

You get better at managing your emotions

You'll become less about you and your child

You become more adept in resolving conflicts and avoiding impulsive responses

Your relationship between you and your child can be strengthened

How can you practice mindful parenting:

Imagine a time when you felt angry or furious with your child. One which you instinctively reacted because this is what the majority people do whenever difficult thoughts judgements, feelings, or thoughts occur. In stressful situations, in which our emotions are rapidly active, it's difficult to be the most perfect person we can be. It is possible that your child will be able to identify the triggers.

If you want to change your behavior You must first be aware of the "hot places" and triggers for emotional reactions. Hot spots are the specific times in our day where we're more vulnerable and less emotional. It is possible to feel over-stressed, tired, stressed or unable to cope or are overwhelmed by our marriage or job.

Emotional triggers are feelings or opinions derived from your education that can arise when your child performs the following actions:

Your child's behavior is in a manner that goes against your beliefs. Example:

Your child throws food out in a restaurant, or picks up all the toys at a shop, making you feel ashamed or embarrassed.

Your child's actions can trigger an old memory or reaction. For instance, your child isn't performing at the academic level you think they should be, and you think you've have failed as a parent because you got a poor grade, you were told by your parents that it wasn't enough.

The behavior of your child could trigger an emotional state or trigger an event. For instance, if you hurt your arm when you were climbing in the jungle gym when you were when you were a child and are scared every time your child goes to the play area.

Your child's actions trigger the eyes of your fears and hopes. For instance: If one of my kids awakes the other in the night, but there's no sleep and everyone is crying I'm afraid I'm missing out on adult time and have completely lost my old self now as a parent.

In order to feel more in having control over the emotions you must first be able to comprehend and predict which circumstances are likely to trigger emotional triggers and hot spots within you.

There are many aspects that are essential that parents must be aware of.

Three key elements of attentive parenting

1. Pay attention to your feelings when you're in a disagreement or with your kid:

Take a look at your latest disagreement or unpleasant situation in your relationship with your child. What emotions are you experiencing? Are you angry, humiliated or embarrassed? Do your best to feel your emotions or feel it as waves that are appearing and then disappearing. Do not try to stop or block the emotion. Do not try to push it away. Don't be a judge or reject it. Don't try to keep the feelings about. Don't hold onto it. Don't try to make it bigger than it is already. It's not your feelings and don't need to respond to the emotion. Be present, fully conscious of the situation. Be aware that you don't have to blame yourself or your child on the incident.

Try to view the issue through the eyes of your child. If you don't see any positive qualities in your child in an argument or a tantrum then think of a moment where you felt a connection with your child and reacted with compassion. Try to remember that version of your child every time you're triggered.

While you are going through your day, try to observe when you begin feeling anxious or frustrated. This could be a sign that you're feeling triggered. When you have identified your triggers, it is possible to move on to the next stage.

2. Take a moment to think before you react to anger:

The most difficult and crucial part of mindfulness is the ability to find that peace during the midst in the present. We can practice finding that space by paying attention to our breathing and body because emotions manifest themselves in changes in the body or breathing. When we take a moment to slow down and concentrate on our breathing and our body it triggers a physiological change that decreases our reflexive reflexes as well as increases the abilities that our brain's prefrontal cortex has.

All of this can lead to a more peaceful mind, that allows space to feel the sensation. If we are able to stop in our thoughts, we can feel the emotions as sensations that are felt in our bodies without fueling them with the focus of the trigger. In this area it is possible to take a moment to relax and bring our attention back to the present moment and then decide to respond in the way we would like to and not reacting because we're not in control.

3. Be attentive to a child's viewpoint, even when you do not agree with it.

Your child will behave like an infant! That means they may not always be able to control their emotions. Children are still learning to regulate themselves (really as are a lot of adults) and they have different goals than you do. Their actions will hit your trigger at times and that's fine.

The issue is when grown-ups start acting like children as well. Instead, if we remain focused - that is, that we pay attention to our emotions and let them flow without acting upon them - we demonstrate the art of controlling our emotions, and kids learn by us.

Being able to take a breath before responding takes effort, and the capacity we have to control our emotions is contingent on what's going on in our lives. This is why self-care is essential. It is impossible to pour our entire lives every single day and not take the time to replenish ourselves. Parents often feel guilty about not taking care of their own requirements. This isn't selfishit's vital. You must make yourself a priority because the more relaxed you are your self-esteem, the more confident you will be able to deal with the issues that come up.

It is essential to know how you can help yourself and address your needs for emotional support. Self-care options could include getting a break by staying in the bathroom in case you are struggling with your children (which was what I tried last night) or having some time for taking a deep breath, switching on the TV so that you and your child get an opportunity to write in journals and taking a shower. taking a stroll, or conversing with your friend or partner.

Sometimes we don't manage to control ourselves at the right time, and we react in ways that we regret. In those situations we can apologize to our children after we have yelled at them because we're still learning, and parents do make mistakes also.

Chapter 4: Helping To Maintain Your Tranquil Home And Linking It All.

Five ways to create a peaceful home with children

It's not easy to say my home is tranquil, as we have five kids aged 9, 7, 4 2, and 2 months. However, two years ago, we made conscious changes to our parenting habits that have provided peaceful moments in our everyday day life. Our kids are working, cooking and playing with each other without the constant shouting or jealousy and sibling rivalries that used to disrupt our daily time. Changes in our parenting were difficultas our swift move to homeschooling required my husband and I to be in the same boat regarding our parenting styles and be very aware of our choices as parents. Homeschooling or not any family should enjoy peaceful moments of time together. Peace isn't a desire it's a requirement. If your family wants to be together, love each otherand become an entire family, you have to help them learn how to live peacefully.

These are five strategies that have allowed our family to be more peaceful

1.) Attitude is an individual choice. I say often as if it were an unbroken record "Attitude is an option." We teach our children on the difference between attitude and emotion. It is possible that you are unable to manage your emotions or feelings within, but you can control your attitude. The four-year-old in our family may be overwhelmed by jealousy that his sister got the biggest taco, but he's got to be in control of his behavior and gently ask for a portion instead of taking the food off of her plate.

The time Doctor. Philip was a brand new physician, he shared with me a tale. "I was able to control my temper through trial and error. A baby I spent months caring for in the hospital passed away unexpectedly. I spent two hours in the hospital with the health care professionals who were performing CPR as well as pushing the cardiac medication and trying in saving his life. He passed away. I sat in the family members and wept. When the session was over, I was overwhelmed with patients who had waited for too long to be seen. Disappointed and tired I managed to hold back my tears and went to see the next person. As I was visiting my next patient I was uninterested and said that the family members were offended. The family complained to the doctor regarding my unprofessional attitude, and I ended up getting in trouble. I discovered the horrible truth: it isn't a matter of whether my previous patient passed away, I was required to walk into each room for patients with a smile in my eyes and with a positive attitude". The attitude you choose to adopt is yours regardless of whether the emotion isn't.

If I don't help my children learn how to control their attitude, they will and it won't be very nice. As a type of discipline, they may be required to write essays on the best way to maintain an optimistic attitude. This might sound unnatural, but gaining the art of controlling your attitude is essential to the success of any aspect of life. Children with negative attitudes have a difficult time to keep and make their school friends. Adults who have bad attitudes tend to be the first ones to be fired, regardless of how attractive, smart or competent they are.

Oh, and I need to be mindful of my behavior at home Also, I have to control my attitude at home. If I'm not a cherry my kids throw the blame right back at me, "Mommy, attitude is an option!" They love to repeat this when I am angry, and that brings me to the second spot...

2.) Words could be more damaging than spanking. I do not hit or spank my children however it took me a long time to realize that I can be just as destructive with my words. I've made comments that I could never include on a blog. It was because I believed it really helped my children modify their behaviour. However, changing behavior that results through suffering- emotional or physical - doesn't make for lasting and successful change in behaviour. Parents, as parents need to be polite even when we're angered and angry. Be quiet, or better yet, avoid shouting at all.

Instead of getting angry, you can name the behavior. I have learned this from Sesame St.--there's one instance where Cookie Monster gets accused of lying to the police about the theft of cookies. Disappointed and angry, Cookie Monster responds, "Me is a glutton I'm not a lying liar." When Sesame Street can use terms such as "gluttony" to spot misbehaviour to identify misbehaviour, then I can also. We use words such as "jealousy," "gluttony," "patience," "kindness," "diligence," and "charity." It was strange initially, but now I love it when a 6-year-old says to her brother who is teasing her, "That's not charity!"

Today, we're more adept at imposing penalties without yelling or screams. If there's a hit I simply tell the child, "That's not kindness," and send the child on time-out which is usually in the bathroom (so it's not possible to claim, "I need to go to the bathroom!") Older kids usually have to write an essay that reflects on their behavior while in time-out. Sometimes, we assign additional tasks, require them to do tasks to someone they've insulted or use natural punishments (ie If you write on your clothes you must still wear that dress) (ie If you write on your clothing you are still required to wear the clothes).

Inappropriate remarks about others are not acceptable between siblings, either. There is no room for freedom to express opinions in our household. I'm not convinced that "sticks and stones may cause me to break bones, however words aren't going to harm my feelings." We have sanctions for mean-spirited siblings and ask our children to reflect on why they chose to behave in a negative way. I do tell my children that outside the home, we are entitled to the right to speak freely, and it's legal to speak hurtful things, but we can't retaliate that brings me to the third point...

3.) Eliminate any physical violence, including I observe "rough playing" along with "sibling competition" at the ER every day and kids whose siblings have pushed them out of an over-sized bunk bed, raced through them on bikes or bent their arms while wrestling, etc. The majority of the time, the entire group is in ER and laughing at the incident. However, a broken limb isn't funny to the patient (or parents who are paying for the ER cost) (or their parents that pay copays for the ER cost). A slap, or a hefty push between siblings is an attack. If an activity is forbidden in the outside of the home is not acceptable within the home.

The reality of bullying between siblings is that it can cause physical and mental suffering. A paediatric research study from 2013 revealed that children who face siblings who are hostile to each other have a higher risk of mental illnesses.

We have a zero-tolerance policy against physical violence like kicking, slapping or biting, spitting wedges, pushing pencils through flesh and any else that they could think of. We talk about inappropriate behavior and the consequences that it can have every morning at our family gathering that brings me to the fourth item...

4.) Hold a family gathering every morning: Each school class starting from pre-K to high school, begins with an early beginning of the day "meeting" and announcements. Why? Since stating expectations can reduce arguments and infractions. When our kids were at school, we had their "meeting" inside the vehicle while driving to school every day. Today, as homeschoolers we have it in the living room. We talk about the schedule that we will follow throughout the week, establish expectations for behaviour and clearly define penalties for bad behavior. I'll say to my 4-year-old, "Your brother has a piano lesson starting at 3:00. If you're able to read together with me, without complaining about the lesson, we'll make the Lego dinosaur together once we return at home." Also, we talk about the menu as well as ideas for family outings. Once students are aware of what they can look at, they're determined to finish their day's work. This brings me to the number five...

5.) Plan many fun activities I consider fun activities my source of income as a parent-- my motivation to inspire my children (and my own) to put in the effort. Find something to do with your family every day, even when it's just a great meal and 20 mins of playing with your family Lego building before the bed. I need to make these plans even the dinner. Between dance, soccer and choir as well as scouts, it's difficult to get anything done as a family if you don't plan it. It's tempting to skip family meals due to jam-packed evenings of practice. Each week, we organize a family outing together. The family that plays together remains together. Setting a solid foundation for peace, even though it's not always efficient, will give your children the knowledge and disposition to be able to gracefully manage their relationships with family, friends as well as co-workers, neighbors and bosses as well as powerful figures. Your home will become an incredibly peaceful and a happier- one.

Chapter 5: Understanding About Parenting

Story

Inda is fourth of five children born to the Obakpolors, Mr. and Mrs. Obakpolor. The Obakpolors are widely recognized as responsible Christians in their local area of Benin City.

Linda along with her brothers and sisters were raised by strict home-schooling. Linda was a virgin to at the age of 22.

But, all of the education and education began to disappear when she was introduced to a charming young man named Kingsley who lived close to her home at the moment; one event led to another (as it is often stated). The young man became closer to Linda and they soon began an affair that began being friends for nothing. As time passed, they became closer. Please remember that she was an unmarried woman at the age of 22 when she first met Kingsley.

Before anyone could even say Jack Robinson, Linda got pregnant just a few months into her affair with Kingsley. Linda was too scared to tell anyone about the scandalous event because she was aware that everyone knew she comes from an honest Christian family, and breaking this news could have a devastating effect. Linda was able to decide to go through with an abortion and promised her self that she would never again have sexual relations with Kingsley once more.

But the proximity of Kingsley's home to hers changed this promise into mere words. She began to having sexual relations with Kingsley regularly.

In order to cut the long story short In the space of two years following her meeting Kingsley she had performed around four abortions on Kingsley. The tragic aspect of the tale is Kinglsey was never loyal to her. She was aware of this when she visited him with no prior notice. She then was able to meet another girl in a dangerous situation. Linda was so angry, she shouted her ire at Kingsley and he was equally upset because she was unwilling to hear any explanations he was required to offer. In the blink of an eye Kingsley has already dealt Linda an ax to the head.

The saddest part of the story is that no matter how responsible the parents of Linda were unaware to Linda's adventures with Kingsley. This particular tale is the story of many youngsters that are today coming born into responsible families. We have many parents who can speak to their children's character while they're at home, however it is not known to parents that their children are different when their parents aren't around.

The issues that are mentioned in this story continue to be caused by ignorance on the part of parents who did not follow through with what they were supposed to do and in the method they're supposed to accomplish these things.

Today, the majority of parents do not learn the basics of parenting until they are parents, and that's where the problem lies. There's a saying that "he who does not plan is trying to succeed" and one of the aspects of planning is the subject matter of this chapter about, which is to do with learning the best ways to conduct parenting.

To understand the basics of parenting, it is important to be aware of the different kinds of parenting styles currently in use (two of the most popular styles actually)

1.) Authoritarian Parenting

Parents who are authoritarian are the types of parents who do not let their children speak their minds and are typically extremely strict, so that even when their children do what is right, they don't encourage and reward them any way.

This type of parenting style is often a challenge for children to be autonomous in their decisions. This most often, youngsters eventually becoming irresponsible with their actions.

If you are too strict or rigid an adult and you observe your child being reckless and you're thinking why, take a look for the most likely cause. could be because you've been too strict with the child.

Consider rewarding your child when they exhibit the right or proper behaviour instead of scolding or punishing them for bad or wrong decisions. Encourage her to voice her own opinions and beliefs even if you're not in agreement.

2.) Permissive Parenting

Permissive parents are those types of parents who don't make rules, and typically do nearly everything with their children. Children require their parents to define clear expectations and rules regarding behavior to develop a sense of responsibility.

While it is the duty for parents to help set their children on the path to success the children ultimately are accountable for their own decisions.

If you aren't happy with the behavior of your child, consider examining yourself before focusing on the problem with your child. It could be that there's a place for Improvement in your ability to meet your own obligations for your child.

As a parent You are expected to be aware of and select different aspects of these two parenting styles in order to achieve an appropriate balance in the instruction of your child.

They must make an effort to study Parenting since it is impossible to provide what one doesn't already.

Read books about parenting (just as you read this one) You can also listen to audio or video messages that cover the same topic(s) as well.

No matter where you are in your learning process about parenting, it's not too late to begin studying it through every source you can find.

Be A Role Model To Your Children

T
Here are plenty of parents who take their time and spend a lot of time educating and training their children about what they should do and not do, but pay little focus on their own personality so that it becomes obvious to the children they're trying to educate.

For parents who are like this they do not seem to realize that children often know who their parents are more than what they communicate to them. This is the reason why this hilarious idea of "do what I tell you to do, but don't do what I say" isn't going to bring any real change for the lives of children in the end.

What you wish to observe in your children should reflect the same that you do as a parent.

There are specific areas in which parents need to be role models for their children. Check out these areas below.

1. Self-Improvement

Whatever cliche you choose to use as a parent self-improvement must always be the top priority and this is vital. Take on new challenges and expand your perspective.

It teaches children to never ever stop growing. The ideal attitude to adopt should be the one that says there's never a dull moment to be learned. Therefore, try to be a student of something new and unique every single day.

2. Serving/Volunteering

Create a habit to enjoy a night out with your family , and also volunteer your time and talents to the benefit of other people.

This is among the most effective ways to get your family members feel united and develop the abilities of teamwork, and most of all, to have generous and caring hearts.

We're expected to train our children to be able to meet the requirements of other people. It is not a good idea to have the mentality of simply receiving goods from other people, but instead helping others.

3. Open Your Life

Do not conceal your identity as a person to your children. It's only a matter of time when the truth is able to come out, even at times that nobody would even think about.

Tell us about your experiences (mistakes and strengths and mistakes) so that your children be able to get an idea of who your parents are.

Let them know vulnerability isn't an inherent weakness, but rather a virtue that is derived from being robust. Get your children near you and encourage them feel like they are working with your example and allow them to see the things you do every day in close proximity. Status isn't a lot in contrast to your attitude, which means lots.

4. Self-Control

The moment we let our emotions go regardless of what they are it is generally healthy and can help reduce stress in general. But, the way we do it when we are with children could result in serious consequences, especially in the event that it is not done properly.

It is vital to learn self-control as often as is possible before our children, regardless of how difficult it may seem.

It is crucial to master controlling your temper. If necessary remove yourself from the situation that is trying to get for you to be a bit agitated, so that you can settle down slightly to avoid making a wrong decision.

5.Respect and listening

The best method to teach your children to be confident is by giving them respect for who they are , and taking note of what they're saying that is on their minds.

It's not an easiest type of leadership however, the most effective leaders pay attention and speak more. It is essential to be open with your thoughts and listen to what your children are saying to you. They'll then be able to follow the same path in the future, it's how things work in general.

6.Goal Setting

Goal Setting is crucial as it gives us a reference point or a sense of where we're headed and the progress we're making. The implementation of the goal and reaching the goals is equally crucial.

If our children see us as parents who are moving along and going about things in general accordance to schedule, it shows them the importance of self-control and organization in their lives.

Encourage them to create your own objectives and to be appreciative when these goals are achieved.

7. Walk the Talk

The most crucial aspect of being the role model your children will have is to make sure you speak the truth and be true to what you say. Be a good role model. As mentioned in the past, it should not be a matter of "do what I say, not do what I say".

Make sure you back up your words by taking action that is obvious and show that you're a man with respect and integrity. They speak louder than words.

"Well done is more effective than saying well." -- Benjamin Franklin

Instructing Your Children

I

It is crucial that parents understand a few essential aspects in the process of educating their children even before they reach their teens.

Let us be aware of the following information as we prepare to teach our children properly beginning in the infant stage.

1) Always allow children to "do the work by myself" as well as "help" even if it's more work for you.

Parents, you must to let your children take on tasks for themselves and help even when it is more work for parents. Young children are desperate to comprehend how they can master their own physical environment and, if given the opportunity to learn they'll be able to take on the role of an individual who is "responseand able." You must be close and collaborate with your child to assist them discover the pleasure of making a contribution. It's more important than performing the task correctly or swiftly. Be aware that you're also creating bonds, which is a factor that allows kids to continue contributing.

2) Rather than simply giving commands Try asking your child to engage in the thinking.

As an example instead of telling the child, instead you can say to the "Brush your teeth!" Are you packing your bags already? Don't forget to pack your lunch!" You could inquire "What's your next step you must do to get yourself ready for the school day?"

3) Teach your child that she must take responsibility for how she interacts with others.

If your child is a nuisance or hurts her brother's feelings, don't pressure her to apologize and insist that she has to apologize. Even if she apologizes then, clearly she won't be saying it out of desperation because she did it in response to your request for her to apologize and it will not help the situation. Instead, pay attention to her thoughts and feelings assist her in sorting out the tangled emotions that caused her shout or cause harm to the brother. Once she's feeling and is feeling a little better then inquire about the things she should have done differently to improve the relationship between them.

Perhaps she'll be willing to apologize, or perhaps that may feel like losing face, and she'd rather make amends with him in her own manner by helping him with the chore to set the table, telling him a story, or even giving him a huge hug.

This helps children understand that how they treat other people has an expense, and when they do harm they are accountable for repairs. Since you're not making her apologize or to make the repair it is possible for her to choose to complete repairs that make it feel great and allows it to come naturally, and it makes her more likely to do it again.

4) Don't try to rescue your child from an ensuing situation.

Make yourself available for problem-solving and helping him to work through the emotions and fears he has and to ensure he doesn't simply ignore the problem, allow him to take the initiative regardless of whether it requires giving an apology or an changes in a tangible way.

5) Model accountability and responsibility.

Make clear and concise the choices you've made.

You must adhere to the promises you gave your child and don't make excuses. If you fail to keep your word when you say that you will take the notebook for school, or to play the game with him on a Saturday then why is he responsible to keep the promises and commitments he made to him.

6)Remember that no child in their right mind would like to be doing "chores."

Most kids do not be enticed to perform "chores" within the house as those at school. Don't "make" your child perform chores when you're not around until they become an integral element of your family's routine and one that your child is not able to be able to resist.

Your aim should not only be for the work to be accomplished, but rather to shape the child to take delight in contributing and taking responsibility. The job should be enjoyable. Offer all the support, structure and assistance that is required, such as helping him sit with him and, when necessary, helping him for the first 30 times that the job is completed.

Be aware that it's more difficult to do it yourself. Remember that when you do these tasks, there is pleasure in the process. Remind yourself of that, along with the satisfaction that comes from a job which is done with excellence. In the end, he'll be able to complete these tasks by himself. This day will come quicker if he is able to do these tasks naturally, without being required to do them.

7)Kids have the need to make a difference for the common good.

Every child has a contribution to offer to us in a way often. Find the ways to comment on them even if it's simply observing that she is so sweet to her baby brother or the fact that she's always singing. What you make note of and recognize will improve.

As they grow older, their roles are likely to increase in the home, as well as outside. The children need to grow to fulfill two distinct responsibility: contributing to family's welfare as well as their personal self-care.

However, of course you can't expect children to develop a loving and positive attitude in a short time. It typically takes time. You can, for instance, ask toddlers to place dishes on tables. four year olds can make matching socks, and six year olds are prepared to take care of the table. 7 year-olds are able to water plants as well as eight years old are able to fold laundry.

The importance of discipline the Parenting

Parents should create an approach to discipline that grows in severity and includes corrective communications as well as punishment, in order to improve your child's life all over the world. Children are driven to rebel against established authority rules. They want to have their own way. If they're not disciplined, they will eventually be in rebelliousness against God and the constituted authority.

Uncontrolled children are likely to repeat their mistakes and indiscretions. Parents must discipline their children not because they've been irritated and embarrassed but simply because their children did wrong. It requires a lot of effort and determination. A child's discipline requires an organized plan and a partnership with both parents due to its significance.

Parents should expose what the child's actions were wrongfully before the kid. Additionally, it is crucial to clarify what's wrong with the actions and the reasons why it was not right. Short-term and long-term consequences must be discussed with the child as well.

There needs to be a equilibrium between corrective communication and punishment, and this is the most important factor in managing a child's behavior.

There ought to be less reason as children grow older and more punishments so that they are taught to be more disciplined.

It is important to communicate with children and less punishment for children as they get older.

If children aren't taught to obey by their parents via punishment while they are still young they will not be able to be able to react to reasoning or communication as they grow older. It's much more difficult once they're older.

Spankings are generally viewed as a scourge and viewed as barbaric due to the extreme amount of child abuse that is prevalent in society generally. However, any type of abuse, whether physical or not was never a viable option in the beginning.

Take note of these points whenever discipline is being enforced against children.

1.Discipline is not to be used in a state of anger.

Parents who shout and yell on their kids or punish them with anger, it is known as abuse. In most cases, it won't result in the right outcome they would like to observe for their child. Parents must ensure that they are at ease and calm when they are disciplining their child.

2.Discipline must be equivalent to the disobedient or wronged behavior.

Parents should carefully consider the consequences of each violation. If discipline is only partially enforced the child could be in rebellion.

Additionally to that, when the form of punishment to be determined parents need to differentiate between childishness and foolishness.

It's only normal for young children to spill milk. That is what is known as childishness. If they spill milk, it isn't an act of rebellion, nor is it a sign of foolishness. In fact, foolishness is a crime to be punished and childishness must be corrected.

3.Discipline must be consistent.

If a parent keeps telling his children "If you violate this then I'll discipline you at back home" when the parents ignores the child, they discover that the parent may not always mean what he/she says. they say, and as a result they don't have to comply.

If a parent does not discipline the child every time he or she switches on the television when they're sleeping and then decides to discipline their child at the next time this can confuse a child. The discipline must be consistent between parents. Parents should present a united front. Otherwise, it could allow manipulation by the child and lead to discord in the marital relationship.

4. Discipline will create close bonds instead of a gap.

When a child doesn't in line with his parent, gaps are created within the family. If the child is punished by the parent but not punished, it shouldn't result in an even bigger gap, but it should help restore the closeness of the relationships. Parents should not discipline their children when they are angry or use harsh discipline that further isolate the child, instead of bringing him closer.

When establishing a system of punishment for our children, parents must constantly discipline their children by means of communicating with them. They should teach their children the difference between right and wrong, and explain why the wrong thing is incorrect.

To raise responsible Children, Parents should avoid Inciting their Children

When it comes to discipline, it's crucial that parents do not punish children in a manner that causes anger. There are instances when a degree of discipline implemented on the child can cause deep and resolute anger that remains within the child and impacts how he behaves for the remainder the rest of his existence. This anger could lead to anger towards parents as well as the people they are likely to interact with in the world and can prevent children from becoming the responsible person they're expected to be.

What can parents do to influence their children bitter? This can happen in a variety of ways.

1.Parents can make their children unhappy because they don't discipline them.

This is among the fastest ways to create anger in kids. Children who are soiled are unrewarding and bitter. Since they are entitled to their own way every day They become angry whenever an authority doesn't provide exactly what they want, or if life gets a bit challenging for them. Parents can cause them to be angry by failing to drive the naivety or foolishness from their minds by discipline.

2.Parents can make their children angry through abuse or by not imposing proper discipline.

The act of abuse, whether verbally or physically abused, typically creates seeds of anger or hatred into the minds of children. This anger created can be difficult to get rid of. The majority of the time, children are violent towards others because of their anger inside of their own.

But, we can observe this as not only an outcome of abuse but also from improper discipline. If a parent uses his anger improperly, it can teach the child to subconsciously employ his own anger as well. For instance, the parent is angry and then curses at the child, blames him for his actions, or even harshly discipline him. Even if the punishment may be correct, the improper use of anger teaches the child to be a bad person. What the child learned is that it's not a bad thing to curse when angered; it's acceptable to engage in physical fight with someone." He does not learn how to manage his anger under control , and as a result the child continues to battle with anger throughout his entire life.

3.Parents turn their children into unhappy by not taking care of them.

A lot of children are bitter when they join forces because their parents aren't present most of the time.

Therefore, they are not loved and affection, which causes anger in them. Many parents leave their children because of work. They are able to work for all day long to attain a certain level of success. This means they aren't home. This ultimately hurts children emotionally and spiritually.

Unfortunately, in our culture parents tend to leave their children behind by sending their children off to schools or extra-curricular activities. Most of the time, these programs are designed to make up for the lack of involvement.

It is not an appropriate idea for coaches, teachers or babysitters to be raising children. This is the reason why children are left to parents. They certainly have a part to play however, it is crucial that parents play a major role on your children's life. Parents should be cautious not to leave their children in the hands of others.

4. Parents cause their children to be bitter by not helping them or showing them the love they deserve.

Healthy parents don't just discipline their children, but they usually offer them rewards too. Parents reward their children when they perform well, and they discipline them when they commit wrong things. Only by this method of balanced discipline that children can begin to grasp the meaning behind fairness.

5. Parents cause their children to be bitter by showing favoritism towards siblings.

How many times have we observed that siblings get very bitter towards one another due to the fact that their parents were not smart in their parenting style towards them? Children grow up disliking each other. "Mother always believed you were beautiful!" "Dad always liked you for being the smartest and fastest!" This happens all often, when parents irritate their children with comments about preference for one another.

Chapter 6: Ten Parenting Strategies You Should Know For Your Child (Boys And Girls)

If you are a parent, keep in mind that after a couple of years, the same kids will enter a significant stage in their lives, namely, the teens.

This is a fascinating phase of life for a lot of people as this phase of life is a distinct and distinctive one in that it is during this time that the individual involved is not able to declare themselves to be an adult, and in the same way, they are not called an infant.

Thus the necessity of parents taking extra care in training their children at this point is not overemphasized. We should take note of the following suggestions when we start to plan for our children's education throughout their teens.

Story 3

Tolani Awojobi is the sole child of Mr. and Mrs. Awojobi. They were not just responsible Christians but actually preachers to the Gospel (Pastors).

Given the type of individuals that they are, they provided Tolani the highest quality of education that they could afford as they were the only child. They made an effort to teach and supervise her to the highest of their ability, especially in the time Tolani entered her teens.

When Tolani was just 16 years old, the son of the Landlord who owned the house where they lived at the time , known by the name of Segun was close to Tolani since they were at the same grade in secondary school. However at different schools.

The other day Mrs. Awojobi was shocked to see her daughter playing with Segun close to the house. Surprisingly to Tolani her mother, she became annoyed at her. She was wondering what the reason for her anger as in her eyes, as her perspective, she did nothing wrong. She was simply an innocent discussion with a colleague, and the relationship between them was purely platonic.

In her surprise and shock to her shock and surprise, the mom didn't just yell at her, but she also proceeded informing her husband Mr. Awojobi that he must be aware of the manner in which their daughter was laughing sexily with the boy. She also stated that this is the way to begin a reckless lifestyle for a girl as she starts to dance and laughing unnecessarily around a boy. Tolani's father was also with his wife to slam Tolani. He asked her why she behaved in such a reckless manner with regard to the family she comes from. Tolani's question that nobody can possibly answer and provide an answer to was when did innocent laughter and chatting between two people (both teens) turn into an act of irresponsibility?

Tolani did not stop considering this issue for a long time until she made a bad choice prior to being accepted to the University. Tolani claimed that her parents believed that she was in fact interacting with a guy, when actually there was nothing sexually intimate between them or even a kiss. And furthermore, she was in a relationship that was not even a couple to the point of being a virgin. One of the mistakes she made was that when she goes into the University she would reveal to her parents with her actions the true standard of irresponsible living, because they deemed her irresponsible even though she was innocent. She chose to live in a bad way once she was accepted into university. University Campus.

Then, a few years later, and by the time Tolani graduated from University, she had a single parent with two kids with different fathers.

The reality of the tale you've just discovered is that this is the sort of reality that present in our modern society. Many children who come from homes with a good reputation are terrible at the end the day. In other families, what turns out to be bad could be due to the fact that the daughter was pregnant and then became a single mom, but for some, the child could be a lesbian or criminal. In different families it could be due to the son turning into a chain smoker or homosexual. However, in the present in the present, the negligence of a lot of parents have led to a lot of reckless children born by responsible parents.

This is the major issue that the book you hold you are reading is trying to resolve. Please take the time to read this chapter thoroughly and make sure you finish it before you return to go back to chapter one.

And, not only that, make sure that you practice every aspect of your life.

After having read this book, the errors that led to the mistakes in the real life stories we've read shouldn't be repeated in our lives or those of our children, and that's the reason for the inclusion of these stories in the book. We are not able to afford making the same mistakes as all the parents.

Please take note of these points when we start to plan to teach our teens in a proper manner from this point from now onwards.

1)Parents must be aware of their children.

Parents need to know their children's names if planning to teach them to be responsible for their lives since you cannot really teach someone you don't know and that's the problems of a lot of parents begins as their children reach their teens.

Scriptures affirms that "Train your child in the manner he is supposed to follow, and when you are old, the child will never change it. Parents can harm their kids by trying to teach their children in a manner that is contrary to how kids are wired.

This could be done by putting their children in areas where the kids do not have any aptitude or enthusiasm for.

God has given us children with are a distinct and unique program, just like computers. It is not possible to utilize the same Software specially designed specifically for the Apple PC with a Dell PC, and the same is true for children. Some are wired to art while others are wired for technology and that's just the beginning.

It is the duty of parents to to know how their children learn, so that they can help their children in these areas.

This could be difficult for parents, particularly in the event that their child's behaviour does not match with their ideals or what they see as a successful person in society. If parents wish to learn about and comprehend their children and the way they're wired, they need to make time and spend quality time with their children. Similar to how the husband and wife must spend time together in order to nurture and strengthen their relationship Parents must spend quality time with their children as well. This isn't always easy as increasing the amount of kids increase. Many parents have found a way to get around this issue by scheduling times (either monthly, weekly or both) for each child.

For example, on a Monday night dad will take his daughter out for dates, or perhaps once per month, on Friday nights, mom will give her son an opportunity to indulge in their favorite restaurant.

Parents must make time together with children to talk to them, to learn from them, and enjoy themselves with them in the end, for the purpose of helping them become responsible adults in general.

What can you do to strategically take time to meet your children in order to better guide them in their particular area of interest? It has been stated that a personal connection with a teenage daughter or son is the basis for educating someone correctly.

Many parents have made mistakes in this area because they're quick to inform their children of what they want, without actually having a clue or even trying to collect their feedback at times.

Make your child's confidant and friend so that they can be the first to tell you everything that's happening to them or their. In the meantime, ensure that you're likely to be raising a complete stranger. And by the time you come to meet the real you in your kid, it could be already too to late. Therefore, make sure you begin developing a relationship with your children now so that the actual parenting that produces a positive results will begin quickly.

When it comes to forming a bond with your teenagers Make yourself accessible as a parent, and even when they commit a sin and you are angry, don't scream on them , so that they'll not be able to return to you next time. It is possible to correct through love and this is the only way to produce lasting positive results for teenagers.

2)Use your private (positive and negative) experience to instruct your children.

Today, many parents behave like they did not go through those same teenage years as their children do in the present.

Because of this mindset, parents appear to be too strict when it comes to their children's teenage years, so that they are unable to approach them for advice due to the belief that mommy or daddies will scream at me for the wrong thing I'm doing or did.

As parents, we've experienced a variety of challenges that we have had to overcome the majority of them. Therefore we can utilize the lessons we've learned to help our children learn so that they don't need to make the same mistakes that we made at our young age. It is only possible by ensuring that the truth is revealed to the children at the time they are they are due.

For instance an individual of God brought his beautiful 10-year-old daughter to the very top of his home and she was asked. Do you know what the most important thing you could ever offer me in my life? The daughter replied "No" as the God of God told her that I would like to make sure that when I will be taking across the aisle in your wedding day, you are a virgin no one have ever touched a personal manner. The man then asked her to swear to give him what he's requested?

To the man's delight, the child made a comment that stunned him. Instead of responding to the father's question, she replied, "daddy, as at the time you got married to my mom was you married? Was mum also a virgin? The man was shocked that at first he wasn't sure what to answer the "wonderful inquiry" his beautiful daughter asked. When he finally was able to put his thoughts together, he offered his answer as follows"Daughter, I wasn't not an unmarried woman when I got married to your mum , nor was your mother was a virgin at the time I married her. The reason is quite simple. We had no parents who could train us in as we are planning to educate you now.

The message is that as parents, we need to be sure to tell our children in their teens the complete truth about ourselves in the method of teaching their children to become responsible. one of the main reasons for telling the truth is

for them to understand the mistakes we made so that they don't repeat the mistakes we made as God's man God explained to his daughter.

3)Never refer to your child as "Irresponsible"

Don't label the child you love with the label of "Irresponsible," because the perception we have of our children can be self-fulfilling prophecy. Instead of doing this what you need to do is teach him the various skills required to be responsible in the world. If he's at risk of being constantly lost for example, what you should to to instruct him that whenever the time comes for him to leave, the place he's at, whether that's your house with a friend at soccer practice, in school, and so on. He should then take note of all the things need to be brought to home and ensure that they are completed.

4) Create an All-No-Blame Household.

Most people naturally tend to blame others when something goes wrong. It's as if removing blame could prevent a repeat of the issue, or let us off the hook. However, it is a fact that blaming causes everybody defensive, and more likely to look over their shouldersand to take on a threatening posture rather than making amends.

This is the main reason that children deceive their parents. And, even more importantly when we blame children the blame falls on them to come up with all sorts of excuses that it wasn't their fault, at the very least due to their own understandingwhich means they're not likely to be accountable and, most likely, the issue is likely to repeat in the future.

The opposite of blame is unconditional love. So why do we do it? to make us be less in control and also because we are unable to bear the thought that we may have played a role, no matter how tiny, in the problem. If you're tempted to blame someone else, look once more. Instead simply accept the responsibility that you are able to accept at that moment. It's not a bad idea to stress your responsibility without being too critical of yourself. The best solutions are realized when decisions are made from a place of acceptance rather than an attitude of blame.

5)Teach your children that they do not just are entitled to being an individual, but also an obligation to be one.

It's been demonstrated through studies that those who take responsibility in any given situation are the ones who view themselves as wanting to be different and stand out.

distinct. This is the type of teenagers you'd like to bring up.

6) Strong marriages add stability to the Life of a Child

I often get asked the question "Which conferences should I plan first - a marriage or the parenting conferences?" Without hesitation I answer, "A marriage conference. If couples' marriages aren't very stable the parenting of their children will most likely be in poor shape." It's feasible to have children if your marriage is stable but it's almost impossible when you're in a relationship that's not stable!

You can strengthen your relationship.

7) Parents Should be on the same page

A major cause of discord in many marriages has to do with be related to the child rearing. In order to raise children effectively, both father and mother must stay on the exact and on the same page. Parents need to ensure that they're in sync with regards to their decisions based on their children's needs.

The children of today are so intelligent that if parents aren't in accord the children will masterfully manipulate to achieve their goals and this will impact the goal of raising them to be responsible kids in the future.

8)Protect Your Children

In a world that is filled by humanistic ideas sexual immorality and insanity, pedophiles, and fake teachers, to name the few. It is essential that parents individuals take on the responsibility of taking proper care of children. Parents must be able to ensure their children's safety by giving them the truth in as to be able recognize the those who are trying to influence their thinking. Parents are aware they have their duty to guard their mind or train their child, and not the only the duty of the church. It is their primary responsibility!

Parents should safeguard their children by making sure they are able to control the content they watch on TV as well as what they browse on the internet, and also overseeing and regulating the use of mobile phones, and examining the content as well as books that are utilized in schools. They must also ensure that their children are safe from the kind of society that is full with pedophiles, by making sure that they're not allowed to spend time with any person (even family members or friends) they don't have confidence in or know. Another aspect of protection is that it includes the training of children to be able to resist and report any contact that is not appropriate.

9) Pray for your children

The importance prayer for the children of your family is usually ignored. There are many kids today that are in need of prayers from their parents, but parents don't realize that prayer is vital.

The purpose of praying for or blessing the child you love is to send an intention that has to them a high-value and envisions the future they will have and a commitment as a parent to assist your child achieve that. Be sure to take the time to pray and bless each child.

10) Understand Your Child's Most Important Need

To understand the most important need of your child begins by acknowledging their biggest issue. The main issue is that they were born sinners by nature. Your children didn't get into the world following God. They are just like everyone else someone who is a sinner and needs salvation! The desire to sin is a driving force in their hearts and minds. The issue that is the most pressing for every child is that of salvation, which can only be achieved through a connection to Jesus Christ. Parents must be able to be able to discern whether their children have a personal relationship to Jesus Christ or not.

Don't simply conclude or believe it is your kid who is Christian. The evidence of the new birth can be seen by your child's behavior when you observe the way in which his or her thoughts, life and behaviour begin to focus on Jesus Christ. The birth of Jesus Christ is distinctive and recognized by its results not only through making a choice. The desire to please God is the primary quality and character identical to the character of Jesus Christ. It isn't to say that your child isn't capable of making mistakes, however, he or she should be able to demonstrate a genuine salvation.

However, this isn't attained if parents aren't saved, and also because no one can offer what he doesn't have. Once you've solved your own issue of relationship with God and your family, you should be sure to help your child in the same way regarding their personal relationship with God too.

Chapter 7: Speak The Right Things To Your Children

Being a positive conduit -- a real positive that is not poisonous is a feat that requires a lot of strength. For one thing it's possible that focusing on the negative aspect could be a way of protecting yourself in the event that you are able to anticipate the bad things, maybe you'll be less wounded when it happens. Being compassionate, kind and optimistic could seem risky, as that you're open to suffering.

However, as anyone who has discovered the courage to conduct themselves with positivity will inform that that when we're able accomplish this, it brings dividends. The actions, words and attitudes are a source of ripples, and our positive behavior can affect a multitude of people during the course of the day. It's a lesson we should showing our children.It's especially important to reinforce the importance of positive thinking to our children in the wake of the era of adversity. It's been a difficult past few years, particularly for a child which is why encouraging happiness and warmth in your family is essential. One method to do this is through positive affirmations to children. While it might appear to be an unimportant gesture, positive words could have a lasting effect on your young children. Children are sponges, and you don't know what phrases they'll take on and keep for years after saying it or repeat for themselves in order to through tough moments, or possibly passing it to their friends, hoping to pass on the joy.

These are positive and encouraging things you can talk to your child daily to ensure they are aware that you're always there for them.

1. "Have an awesome day!"
It's a great way to start your day off in a positive way by saying goodbye to your kids in the morning.

2. "Let me think on this."
The best option instead of resolutely refusing to your kids' requests (given that the demands aren't ridiculous).

3. "What has happened?"
Instead of blaming others or jumping to conclusions, e.g. when you find out that furniture that you have in your home has been damaged.

4. "It seems like you're having a difficult time. Do you have any information to share about it?"
This is an excellent way to get your kids to talk to you.

5. "I'm sorry."
If you've made an error Make sure you're humble and take a moment to apologize.

6. "Your practice pays off."
Teens and children are happy when parents see the results of their hard work. outcomes.

7. "How did you accomplish this?"
This can help your children to focus on the process rather than the outcome and is one of the best things you can ask your child.

8. "What's an interesting event that took place in the your school this morning?"
If you ask your kids this question They'll be more likely to talk about their experiences rather than you askingthem "How did your day go?"

9. "What did you do to work to achieve this morning?"
This will remind your children that working hard and advancing is more important than achieving a specific final.

10. "I'm certain you'll succeed. it."
The next thing you could say to your child is "I'm sure you can succeed." Speak this to your children to help them gain a sense of confidence.

11. "You decide."

Children are taught to make rational judgements through making more choices and not following the advice of authoritative individuals.

12. "How are you feeling about it?"
This question will allow your children to become self-aware and emotionally aware.

13. "I'm willing to listen."
If you can assure your children that you're open to listening to them without judgement and they'll be more enticed to speak out what's on their minds.

14. "I adore you."
Teens and children must feel loved and accepted by their parents.

15. "You bring me joy."
If you say this it will brighten their day.

16. "Your perspective is vital."
Children will be able to feel valued when you tell them this. them. If they feel valued it will influence their behavior. It's a

must to be on the list of ways to talk to children.

17. "You were correct."
Be honest when you're wrong. This is among the most effective ways to gain your child's trust.

18. "I can see that you're getting bigger ..."
To find more positive phrases to tell your child make sure to fill in the blanks by using "focused", "organized", "kind", "responsible", "helpful", etc. When you observe even small positive improvement in your child's behavior.

19. "I'm happy to do it along with you!"
This shows the children you really enjoy having fun together.

20. "That's an outstanding question."
Student and tutor working on homework
If you encourage your children's curiosity, you'll instill an attitude of learning for life in your children.

21. "I accept you for who the way you're."
Parents want their children to be confident and secure. Informing your children about this is a great way to guide them down the right path.

22. "You're an essential member in our extended family."
If you're not sure what to tell children be sure to remind them regularly of their significance and importance as members within the extended family.

23. "I am a believer I am in you."
Your children need to know that they trust them, that you trust their character and abilities.

24. "I noticed that you were working very hard in ..."
This phrase demonstrates that issues are something to be accepted, not something to avoid.

25. "Let's take it one way."
Let your children know that your method isn't the sole (or most effective) method.

26. "Can you tell me why you chose to do this in this manner?"
Let your children be reflective about their choices as well as about what they're learning.

27. "You're learning to ..."
Make sure your children are reminded that the joy that learning brings is the one thing that matters the most.

28. "That was kind of you."
Recognizing your child's good attitude and behavior means for them.

29. "Can you demonstrate to me how? ...?"
Your children will gain confidence once they realize that you can learn from them, too.

30. "Good point."
As your children progress into the realm of wisdom and intellectual development let them know that you see this growth.

31. "I believed you could accomplish it."
The words you say to encourage your children allow your children to believe in their abilities.

32. "How did you come up with this?"
Teens and children who think through this process will develop the ability to solve problems faster.

33. "Would you like to have a discussion to me?"
This question is engaging without being overwhelming or demanding an essential part of things you can ask your child.

34. "What do you want to face?"
girl kicking football during practice
It's through challenges that we learn and grow Therefore, this is a good way to teach your children to look at the problems in a positive light.

35. "I take care of you."

If you are embarrassed by telling your children your love for them is unconditional, you can start by saying this instead.

36. "What do you think you can do to fix this?"
Instead of discussing the issue with your children, you can consider asking this question to encourage them to resolve the issue themselves.

37. "Will you be able to forgive me?"
Instead of apologizing, asking your children's forgiveness is an effective method of reestablishing the bond between parents and children.

38. "Tell me about it."
This is a straightforward sentence that encourages children to express their thoughts and feelings.

39. "It's okay for you to be feeling..
Instead of telling your children not to feel sad, angry or upset. Let them feel their

feelings and allow them to deal with the unpleasant emotions.

40. "Shall we begin once more?"
If a fight has broken out between your children and you You can ask this question to begin the discussion again.

41. "I'm happy to be your mother."
If your kids realize that, they'll be eager to show you their pride too.

42. "What could I do in order to become more of a good parent?"
Be ready to receive an honest answer by your kids. When you put their suggestions into action, you'll become an improved parent.

43. "That's an interesting idea."
Your children will see that you are concerned about their opinions and encourage their imagination and self-expression.

44. "That was an incredible act of courage from you to do that."

Change can be a daunting experience. Be proud of your child's bravery and they'll be more confident taking on new challenges.

45. "It's acceptable to not say"no."
Instruct the children how to be tolerant at when they are young. They'll grow into strong individuals who can establish acceptable boundaries.

Encourage your children by using phrases father and child or mother and child gardening together Being a parent isn't simple , but I hope this list of ways to talk to your kids will encourage them, and also helps you build an improved relationship to them!
Use a few of these positive words each week. Be aware of any changes you observe in your children's.

Be sure to take care of your children who have difficult feelings
Children discover emotions through doing things, learning new behaviours, and receiving feedback from their peers.

In helping your child be aware of their emotions and recognize their triggers will be the initial step to helping them manage their emotions.

Instructing your child about why they experience a certain way and why it is so can help them manage difficult emotions.
If a child is able to draw the connections between their thoughts as well as their feelings and their actions it is less likely to be affected when rough emotions surface.
Children learn about emotions the same way as they acquire other skills such as writing, reading and riding bikes or controlling bladder size through trying out new things, forming the new habit, as well as receiving feedback from others in their environment.

Similar to the other things that children are taught control of emotions are more easily acquired by certain children than others. The ability to learn these skills from a variety of sources, such as siblings, parents or friends, as well as from the media, can allow children to learn useful and less effective strategies to control their emotions. As parents, your job is to help your child to practice the coping techniques that are most effective.

Let your child understand the emotions they are feeling.
The first step to help your child regulate their emotions is to teach your child to be aware of the signs of emotions. A great tool to use is the "feelings listing". This is a set of phrases or terms that can be used with a child to discuss their feelings and bodily sensations. If you are experiencing a difficult emotion such as anger, the list could include terms like "sad", "scared", "mad" or "confused" and words to describe emotions in various parts of the body like "tight", "shaky", "pain", "sweaty" and "heart", "stomach" or "hands". These terms for sensations could be especially beneficial to younger youngsters, who may be more comfortable talking about their heart-pounding fast or clenched fists

as an example, and not think about what they're thinking or feeling or.

You can choose the words that are most appropriate for your own personal sentiments list. Make sure, however, to include positive words on the list, like "excited", "glad" or "proud" to ensure that both of you can also enjoy times where things are going smoothly.

Once your child is comfortable with the chosen phrases and words, help your child to utilize them to alleviate any negative feelings, especially when you observe a marked change in their behavior. Keep in mind that regardless of the words spoken by a child it is important to always listen and ensure that the communication channels are open.

Help your child recognize the reasons behind uncomfortable emotions.

When your child tells you about what's happening You can then help them in understanding the reason why they are feeling the way they do. The process of identifying the trigger or cause of emotion could be a challenge for a child, but you can help them understand it by making them honest with themselves and you.

Any time, weeping is a normal response to feeling overwhelmed by intense feelings that include tension, fear, anger or even excitement. However, some children tend to cry more than other children. The same children may also become frustrated more often, be more annoyed, and become too excited compared to their peers too.

The ability to control the most intense emotions is largely determined by age and development. Being more sensitive to things can be a part of what makes someone.

Large emotions can create slightly more difficult for children who are just beginning to become proficient in the management of emotions. Although this can be taught naturally over the years, there are strategies that can help your child develop emotional awareness and implement appropriate coping strategies.

Learn to teach your child about emotions.
Your child should be able to understand and articulate the way they feel.

1 Begin to educate children about emotions, so that they are aware that emotions that appear ambiguous or overwhelming are referred to as.

Tell the world, "You seem unhappy right this moment," or "I can sense that you're angry." Be honest about your feelings as well by saying, "I am sorry that we aren't able to see Grandma this afternoon," or "I'm startled at how these guys could be rude today."

You can also start discussions on emotions through talking about characters from books or in TV shows. Every now and again you can ask questions like, "How do you think the character is feeling?" With practice, your child's capacity to identify their emotions will grow.

The ability to recognize emotions can help children develop psychologically stronger even when they feel intense emotions.

Learning to build an Emotional Vocabulary

Separate feelings from. Behaviors
It's equally important for children to be taught the art of expressing their emotions in a way that is acceptable for others. Shouting in the supermarket or throwing an outburst at school, as an example isn't considered acceptable.

Let children know that they can be triggered by any emotion they wish, and it's fine to be angry or scared. However, be clear that children have choices in how they respond to these painful feelings.

Although they are entitled to be angry with somebody, for instance but that doesn't give the right to hit them. In the same way, toddlers could be disappointed when the store has run out of their preferred ice cream, but that doesn't mean that it's acceptable to scream on the floor and shouting at other children.

Discipline behavior however, not emotions. For example, "You are going to be kicked out of the house because you hit his brother" as well as "You have lost this item for the remainder of the day due to the fact that you're screaming and it is hurting my ears."

Make sure that your child is correct in their behavior Do not correct their emotions. Validate and Relate
Sometimes , parents are unaware of a child's emotional state. By saying "Stop being so angry. It's not that big of a deal" tells your child that their feelings are not appropriate. It's okay to feel emotions, even if you think they are untrue.

If you think they're angry, sad or angry, sad or embarrassed identify the emotion. Also, demonstrate that you can understand the feelings of your loved ones and compassionate.

If you are expressing "I believe you're angry we're not attending the playground today" indicates that you are in a state of anger, it might seem a little rude.
You can instead say, "I know you are upset that we're not taking you out to play today. I'm annoyed when I'm not allowed

to do the things I'd like to do as well." This added element will remind your child that everybody experiences certain emotions sometimes, even though they're not as intense.

While you're at it help your child recognize that feelings are temporary and what they are feeling now will not last for long, or even longer than just a few minutes.
Being aware that emotions, and tears, aren't permanent could help young children remain more calm in the midst of an emotional time.

Show Acceptance
It's not uncommon to have difficulty when trying to figure out how you react to children who are extremely emotional. It's not uncommon to feel overwhelmed or confused by the whole situation.
Although you might not be able to understand why your child feels this way It might be helpful to acknowledge that you recognize they are experiencing certain emotions and it's okay.

Children must be taught to recognize, understand and manage the emotions they're experiencing and being "seen" and embraced can be a huge help.

Some might call highly sensitive children "wimps" or believe that their sensitivity could be cured and that is not only dangerous, but also inaccurate. Being angry, crying and being angry are not necessarily harmful or signs of insecurity. Everybody has a unique personality and sensitivity is only the one you can give your kid. Make sure your child knows that you respect the person they are as they are.

Teach Emotion Regulation
In the realm of controlling emotions, the ability to manage important emotions is largely dependent on the child's age and growth. As soon as a child reaches the age of 24 months old, or sometimes at 36 months, their ability to regulate their behavior is typically low.

It doesn't mean that you shouldn't teach children how to manage their emotions, however. When they enter preschool, a lot of children possess the skills needed to start developing the skills handle their feelings.

Here are some methods to help your child learn to manage their emotions:

Learn to deep breathe. Learn to teach your child how to breathe slowly and slowly through their nose , and then exhale through their mouths. (Try asking your child to "smell the scent of a flower and then blow up the balloon" to master this.) Try this a few times throughout a time of stress, but also you should encourage them to use this independently as needed. Use counting to relax. Learn to distract your child her mind from distressing thoughts by counting. Ceiling tiles that are numbered and counting to 10, as well as counting from 100 to 10 are but one of the many mental games that can ease anxiety.

Have a break. Let your child give his self a few minutes of time out or request a teacher to let them can leave the classroom to drink a glass of water or an hour of quiet when they need to take a moment to think. It is important to inform your child that they have the ability to take this step before they could be detained in case of misbehavior. After that, they'll be the ones to decide the time when they're ready to go out.

Create a kit to help calm your child. Make sure to pack a container with items that can help your child relax (or make them smile) (or to cheer them up). Coloring books, crayons and coloring books stickers that scratch and sniff, pictures that your child likes as well as soothing tunes are just some of the options that can stimulate their senses, and aid in helping them manage their emotions.

Find a solution with your child. If your child's moods are creating problems for them, maybe nobody wants for them as they cry constantly or they're not able to take part in physical education since they're upset when they fail--let them work together to fix the issue. Request their opinions regarding the strategies that could help. They could come up with innovative solutions with your assistance.

Identify mood enhancers. Talk to your child about what they do when they are happy like playing outside or reading a comic book or singing their favorite songs. Record these things down and explain to them that they these are "mood boosters." If they're struggling encourage them to take part in one of these activities to help them deal with their emotions.

Strategies to teach anger management Skills to children
Beware of reinforcing outbursts by repeatedly reinforcing them
How you react to your child's feelings will make a significant difference. Many parents do not realize that they are encouraging their children to engage in emotional outbursts. If you're aiming to

help your child manage their emotions it's best to steer clear of:

Rewards your child for calmness If you give your child with a unique reward each time they pull themselves together, they might discover that crying or yelling at their child is a fantastic way to accomplish the thing they've always wanted.

Doting your child with love If you want to offer comfort, make certain that you don't go overboard. Don't want your child to be taught that getting angry is the best method of attracting your attention.

Reducing your child's anxiety constantly is essential in providing the comfort you need, but it's important to teach your child the techniques they'll require to be able to calm themselves to be able to manage their emotions even when you're not around to help them.

Reminding your child to quit crying. Telling your child to stop crying may make them feel more miserable. And if your children observe you getting angry over their crying and their crying, they might think they're wrong, and that isn't going to make it any easier for them to stop crying.

Informing your child that he or she is sensitized: If you inform each teacher, coach or friend's parent about your kid's sensitive nature, you could send a message to them that they're not able to manage their own emotions. While it's beneficial to give an insights into your child's personality however, it's not an obligation. You should only share this information when you think it can give you any information or help them alter their behavior while playing with your child. Make sure to keep the conversation positive by saying things like "My child is overwhelmed by emotions."

It is likely that there will be instances when it is sensible to shield your child from traumatic events. If you are aware that a depressing film is scheduled to be shown at a sleepover as an example, you could suggest that your child drop out if you're sure that they'll be struggling to come back together after having seen the film.

However, shielding your child from all difficult situations or from all the difficulties of life isn't productive. To be successful and enjoy the benefits living, the child requires some knowledge of how to handle a variety of emotions in certain situations.

You might be thinking about having your child take a break from an event at school because you are aware that they will have difficulty controlling their anger, and you're worried they'll be agitated in the event that their team loses at the kickball competition. Although it might seem appealing however, this scenario will likely to occur at least once in your life, and having experience in dealing with it can be extremely useful.

You must give the children with enough time to deal with their emotions without shielding them from all difficult things. Be guided by your instincts as to what you think is right for your child.

When to seek help from a professional

Although learning about emotional regulation begins at the age of infancy Research suggests that children typically wait until the age of 8 or 9 years old before they can have any real control over it.

4 Therefore, it's highly likely that even kids who aren't typically emotional in nature might experience a period of time when it seems like tears are constantly falling or when they're bursting into rages frequently.

While it's not likely that there's an underlying cause for concern, it's worthwhile to talk with your physician to confirm there's no cause for the symptoms you're experiencing (for instance an untreated ear infection or another medical issue or a mental issue) (for instance an undiagnosed ear infection or a medical condition or a psychological problem). This is especially important in the case of a child who is very small and is having trouble communicating.

If your child has always been emotionally inclined There's no reason to be concerned. However, if they suddenly show more trouble controlling their emotions, consult your physician.

Also, you should seek out assistance from a professional when their moods are causing problems in their life. If they're crying so often during the day that they're not able to concentrate in class , or if they're having difficulty keeping friends because they're not able to control the anger in their lives, then they might require some extra help.

Research has revealed a connection between dysregulation and a variety of mental health issues as children grow older. These range from sadness, anxiety and addiction to drugs to thoughts of suicide and ADHD, attention deficit (ADHD) and even violence.

The good news is that experts believe interventions that target self-regulatory behavior could assist children to develop more.

When a mental or physical issue has been identified it is possible to take the necessary steps to help your child be able to manage their emotions during crucial occasions so that it doesn't cause problems as they get older. If you need help learning how to do this best for your child, speak with the child's caregivers.

It is important to keep in mind that controlling your emotions is a process that requires awareness and capabilities that are in the process of learning. Although, for certain children, being emotionally overwhelmed is a natural tendency.

A little more support along with a little direction and patience from you could be all they require to master managing their emotions in the right way. It can be very challenging at times, however the effort your put in could help your child throughout the rest of their lives.

Be aware that there is an important benefit to this kids with high levels of emotion often experience every emotion vividly. So, even though your child who is extremely emotional might be a victim of intense anger however, they can be extremely compassionate or an incredibly passionate leader. Although people might feel anger at 10 levels however, they might be thrilled and excited at that point too.

Common triggers could be a fight with a sibling or brother or perhaps a poor experience in school or fear or anxiety. Keep in mind that every child is different and something that may not irritate one child may be a significant reason for other. If your child feels upset or scared, let them know that it's normal. You can also explain to them that understanding the root of their emotions can help them to better find other strategies to address similar triggers in the near future.

Help your children manage their feelings
If your child is able to recognize their emotions and the source and the reason for them, you can help them to

understand that they are in control regarding how they handle difficult emotions. A good way to deal with difficult emotions is to help your child create a story that demonstrates the connection between their feelings and beliefs and behavior. If a child does this, they will be able to understand that emotions have reasons and that there's multiple ways to address a problem.

It is possible to help your child to write a narrative of the negative feeling by asking them to describe what happened and what they thought about was happening, how they experienced (including sensations in their body) and then what they thought or did following. This method is particularly effective for children who are younger and require more prompts to create a narrative of their emotions using smaller steps. You can also help your child to express their emotions by speaking openly about your own feelings and how you deal with your own emotions.

If a child is able to draw the connections between their ideas the way they feel, their emotions and their actions They are less likely to be affected when their emotions are triggered. This is because the child develops the ability to think about the triggers that cause them and, with time will determine what they could be able to improve on in the future.

Chapter 8: Supporting Your Kids

Being able to effectively assist your child is difficult for any parent at times. Certain days are more easy than others. The everyday challenges and more long-term stresses such as poverty, violence, or abuse, can cause you to be unable to react to your child in the way you'd like.

Although you're doing your best to become a good parent to your child it can feel like you've been shut in front of you and you're doing everything wrong. Your relationship will shift and becoming more equitable as your children get old and spend more of your time with them. However, this doesn't mean that you shouldn't keep in touch and provide the help they require while they undergo the process of becoming a new person, a mature adult.

This could be helpful if you are trying to figure out why your child requires your support and are interested in learning more about ways to help your child through the teenage years.

What is the definition of supportive parenting?

Being a responsible parent means taking your child's best interests in mind while being active, present and supportive. It involves:

actively helping them achieve their highest academic performance as well as their hobbies and interests, listening without judgement and trying to comprehend their issues and challenges

by praising their accomplishments and encouraging them in their mistakes and difficulties

by providing consistent expectations and penalties in order to make them be confident and predict outcomes, while also developing a relationship of trust.

What makes having a caring parent so crucial for teens?

The influence you have on your child is more dependent upon a trusting relationship than in the amount of power you exercise and the amount of lectures you give. They may appear to be trying to disengage from you however, they're actually trying to elude your direction to take a different path through life, and also to establish a sense of them as an individual and independent individual.

The love, support, trust and confidence from their families make children feel secure and secure. They also serve as powerful tools against the pressure of peers, life's challenges and failures.

Strategies and tips for assisting parents
Your aim is to keep your child secure and provide them with the fundamentals needed to succeed. As a minimum, they should to know that they are valued for the person they are and that you will always be available to provide them with in a safe and secure environment. like a secure and healthy environment to live in as well as healthy food and school supplies are an absolute priority. They need

protection and help to protect them from physical and mental abuse.

respect for their feelings and seeks to acknowledge their birthdays, achievements and other milestones like birthdays or their first day at school . Respect for their peers, their dress as well as their music and sports preferences and interests.

Many parents are struggling to adapt to the responsibilities that parenting their child through the teenage years brings. This can put the most steadfast and most loving relationship to the examination. Your child needs you now as they've always wanted you, only in a completely different way.

They're turning to you for help through one of the most significant changes in their lives toward independence and maturity. If you've experienced it, you're aware of how confusing and difficult the process can become. Don't be afraid to share some of your own teenage experiences with your child. Let them know that you are understanding that it was something you experienced as well. Discuss with them how you dealt with the situation (or failed to overcome it) in addition to what learned from it. Recognizing that everyone faces similar challenges can be extremely comforting for your child, especially in the case where their parent is telling their story.

Your child is developing into an independent individual. They need a strong base of expectations and beliefs that will guide them in the present as they transition into adulthood. Determine what is essential to your family and determine how you'll communicate those values and values to your child. So they'll have necessary information to in their journey through life and make decisions that are aligned with the values of the family.

There's no doubt that the teenage time will surely bring some tension and discontent. There are times that you feel like there is no way to know about your child or are not happy with certain of their choices. Be as compassionate and supportive as you can throughout their difficulties, no matter how small they may seem. If you are able to do this, they'll be more likely to trust you. to talk about their issues and reach out to you whenever they need help.

Make sure you are there for them in the same way that you would have wished your parents to be there for you as you were growing to be.

It might be beneficial to examine the role played by parents in the education of their children to guide the child in the right direction.

Parents' responsibilities can be divided into three main categories:
(1) the role of parents in showing support for their child's educational.
(2) the parental role in making their home an ideal learning environment and also,
(3) the role of parents in helping their child in helping with homework. In the

description of each issue and a list of suggestions for parents has been provided.

Helping the Education of a Child
According to research conducted of Ronald Ferguson, "Nearly half of a child's growth in school can be attributed to factors that are outside of the classroom, like parental support." Thus, the most important support a child can receive is from parents. They are responsible for ensuring that your child goes to school well-nourished, rested and ready to learn, to setting high expectations of their child. These are suggestions on ways parents can support their child's learning:

* Attendance: A good attendance to school is crucial for academic growth. If pupils miss school, they are unable to attend important lessons. Parents have a say in the attendance of their children, which includes making sure that they are on time for school, and not taking their children out during the course of school.

- Attitudes: Parents must to show a positive attitude about school in general. If parents display a positive attitude towards school, their child will have the similar attitude towards school. Parents should be careful about the way they deal with school issues before their child. If they exhibit a negative attitude towards school, their child could adopt the same attitude towards school.

"Priority": education should be given top priority to ensure that it comes to the top. So, parents should consider education to be their primary concern over all other after school activities.

- Support for children: They need the assistance of their parents. If a child needs help in school or has other specific assignments, it's their parents that they can turn to. Parents must be supportive and help their children. Sometimes, they may require help beyond the home like a tutor for instance.

* Be Active Research has proven that self-esteem and academic achievement are directly related to the positive

involvement of parents at schools. If parents are active in school, it could be a motivating factor for the child. It shows the child that parents believe in the importance of school is paramount.

• Communication. Parents have to keep in touch with the school of their child and keep in contact with the teacher.

A Home is a Good Space for Learning

As the child's first teachers There are a variety of ways parents can take in their homes to make it an excellent place for education.

"Read, Read and and Read The most important things that parents can do for their child's development is by reading with their children, or allow their child to listen to their reading. Parents can also help children to read aloud. It is crucial for children to see how their parent reads. Visits to the library are advised.

• High Expectations for Parents: They must to set high standards regarding their child's behavior and growth.

* Praise and Encouragement If parents praise their children and offer encouragement, they create an effect on the child's motivation as well as confidence that they are a successful student.

*Effort: Teachers should to encourage the importance of effort, as well as achievement.

* Routines: It's important for parents to establish family routines that allow time for homework, completing daily chores while eating meals with the family and having a consistent time for bed.

TV: The parents must to ensure that their children's television is monitored in a manner that is appropriate. It is essential to limit the amount of time children spend watching TV, in addition to the genres of television they're watching. Parents can assist their children in selecting television shows which will help them learn more.

* After-school activities For education to be considered a top priority kids must be limited on the amount of after-school

activities they take part regularly. Although after-school activities like scouting, athletics music, and other activities offer a variety of benefits but it is essential parents remember that education should be the top priority. Parents are responsible to ensure that the other activities they engage in aren't affecting the education of their child.

• Listen. It's vital for parents to be encouraging their child to share their thoughts concerning school. Parents should be attentive to their child and respond with compassion.

* Reward Learning Parents can encourage learning by taking their children to parks, museums or theatres. These activities can be among the most memorable and important experiences for children's learning.

• Monitor grades: Parents have to be aware of the grades of their children. Parents can encourage and celebrate wins, and provide assistance in cases where extra effort is needed.

Helping Homework

As we've said before the majority of children can't succeed in school on their own. They need parental help. One method parents can use to motivate their children is to help students with their homework.

* Create a peaceful space It is essential that children have a safe and secure place to finish their education. It should be a peaceful well-ordered location, free from distractions in the home (television or phone) as well as loud and the loud sound) (television and phone as well as loud music).

"Rewarding Progress: Parents must utilize lots of praise in order to reward outstanding work and effort, and also to show the excellence of their child.

Talk about homework Parents must discuss with their children every day about their homework assignments. Parents should review their child's homework to ensure that it's completed and ask questions to their child about the task.

However, they shouldn't do the homework for the kid.

• Schedules and schedules could be crucial for parents to help their child in creating an academic routine. Parents might also have to support their child, break down the school work into smaller pieces and assist them in preparing for assignments that will last a long time.

Moving and flowing with your children

For instance, kids can prepare their own breakfasts take a shower, dress themselves, clean their teeth and generally get dressed for the day with little or no help from us. They can also clean their rooms and sweep, wash dishes mop, dust and even wash their car. Older people are able to cook simple meals and take care of the children. Self-sufficiency is a way to make a huge difference in time and effort over the course of time.

One calendar. When you're home with more than one child and you have many activities taking place that you have to keep track of including school activities like Christmas shows and parent-teacher conferences, to extracurricular activities like dancing classes, soccer practice or spring concerts. Organise your day by keeping a simple schedule (use Google Calendar) and record all your appointments and events in this calendar, from children's items to your daily activities. If they give you papers from school and soccer calendars add everything to the calendar. After that, a quick glance on the calendar daily can assist you in planning your day.

Toy bins for toys. It's the reality that children are stuffed with toys, and they'll be everywhere. You'll be a mess when you attempt to manage your children with a dictatorial ruthlessness. Instead, let your kids play, but make sure you have plenty of bins that they can throw their toys in after they've finished. Cleaning up afterwards is easy and they can simply dump everything that's on the floor into bins, then move on to the next mess.

There are bins that can be designated specifically for toys (this one is for Legos and this one's designed for stuffed animals and this bin is designed for automobiles) Additionally, there are various general-purpose bins to store things that can't be put in other bins. Don't be overly strict about these bins -- the main goal is to make life easier.

Regular clean-ups. If you're anything like me then you do not like huge spills. Encourage your children to tidy up after themselvesallow them to make some mess, but every at times, remind them to clean up. Make sure you tell that they must clean up before moving onto other activities, such as dinnertime or the time to go to bed. It's best to establish certain times of the day to do cleaning up, like before going to the bedtime or before leaving for school to ensure that the home is neat and tidy during the day.

Quiet bedtime routines. Kids thrive in routine and there is no routine more effective than one that is completed before they go to bed. Set a routine prior to bed which could include cleaning up after taking showers and taking their toothbrushes, changing dressed and reading a good book. Reading to them aloud just before bed is a wonderful idea as it calms the mind after a long day of activities, provides them time to bond and also helps get them to read regularly. It's also something everyone will appreciate.

Prepare the night before. Mornings can be an incredibly stressful period for both parents and children alike However, they don't need to be. Instead, prepare as much as you can the evening before, and let your mornings be more peaceful. I prefer to prepare lunches, have their clothes put on (and mine too) after which they shower, and have their school and homework bags prepared. The morning is all about eating breakfast, some dressing, grooming and putting everything away before heading out the to go out the. It's an excellent way to begin your day.

Don't schedule too much. Sometimes, we schedule things back-to-back to ensure that each minute of the day is scheduled. This causes anxiety and issues. Instead, plan as little as you can in a day and allow enough time between the events, appointments or other activities, to ensure that your day can move with a slower pace. Begin your morning earlier than you should, so that there's no rush and allow yourself enough time to move between activities. A schedule that is more spread out is more enjoyable than one that is crowded.

Set aside family time for your family. Make sure you have time in your schedule where you do nothing apart from spending time as the family. For some families dinnertime is a good choice as everyone comes for dinner as a family and there is no other activity scheduled at that point.

For other days, weekends or even only one day of the weekend, are better. We make Sundays Our Family Day and try our best to not schedule any other events on the day. We enjoy looking for with anticipation. In general, weekends are for our family and so are the evenings. everything is completed on the weekdays before 5 p.m.

Simple clothes. It is best to purchase clothing for your children that are easy to match -Choose the same color scheme so you don't have to keep looking through their clothing to find items that match. Take a look through their clothes every couple of months to clear out items that aren't fitting (kids expand so quickly!) and give the old clothes to charity or relatives (or transfer them to an older sibling). Make sure their wardrobe is simpleIf it's not fitting perfectly in their drawers it's time to dispose of it, or dispose of some other item. Do not overflow your drawers or you'll be unable to find things. Additionally, socks can be difficult to find -- make use of mesh bags with one bag for clean socks, and another for dirty socks. Throw that dirty mesh bag into the laundry and your socks won't get found (or at least it won't happen as often).

Make sure to prepare early.And ensure that you take the time to review the schedule prior to the time (usually the day prior) to determine the events coming up. This lets you prepare for the events and activities ahead of time to ensure that you don't have to be caught up in getting prepared. For instance when you play soccer be sure all soccer equipment including folding chairs and drinks and snacks and such, are prepared for the event ahead of time. Being prepared in advance makes things much easier later.

Always bring snacks. Kids always get hungry. Make sure you're prepared when you're out on the road, be sure to put some snacks in bags. Fruit, crackers, cheese carrot sticks PB&J sandwiches and peanuts, graham crackers and raisins make great snacks for your travels. A lunch box that is insulated and has reused ice packs can help keep the food fresh. Make sure to ensure you have plenty of water because kids are always thirsty. We can't help with the frequent bathroom breaks, however.

Baby wipes and an emergency kit. There will always be mess. Make sure you are prepared. Baby wipes, even if they have stopped diapers, are essential for any mess that may arise. Keep them in an "emergency kit" that could contain medical equipment, reading materials as well as games, towels and even extra clothing and anything else you can think of to be ready for whatever often happens.

Make sure to pack spare clothes. We have a carry-on luggage that is always filled with a few different sets of clothes for each child Good clothes (for the occasion of a party or some other event) as well as regular clothing underwear, socks, and other items. We're always prepared in case of an accident or if they'd like to stay with their parents or cousins while we're out for the party or at something.

Make routines for your week. In addition to regular family time (mentioned above) It's a good idea to create a weekly routine that's written down and posted in a place where everyone can see it. A routine for the week might consist of regular practices, house cleaning day and washing the car day of yard work or errands day, regularly scheduled appointments and so on. This helps to make the routine more consistent for everyone and avoids the possibility of unexpected events.

Connect as family. A regular conversations between family members resolves many problems. Set up regular times where families can discuss family problems. It's a good time to have dinner to do this. Also , you can have a monthly "Family meeting" in which you all sit in a circle and discuss family issues, praise and acknowledge each other, organize for your Family Day, and play games afterward.

Go on dates. If you're having difficulty getting time to yourself with each kid (whether you have a single child as well as more than one) making "dates" could be the best way to ensure that you are doing things together. Create a date for your child at a particular date and time, and together, you can decide what you'd like to do that day. It could be something as simple as like a walk through the neighborhood or in an outdoor park, or reading with your child or playing games on the board and sports or video games. It could also be something more like going out to eat, amusement park or movie. If you have a lot of children, you may need to change dates with the kids.

Make time for yourself and your spouse or husband. It's easy to get distracted by your kids that you don't think about your partner. Beware of this occurrenceit's a sure-fire way to break up and lose the connection which brought you to start an entire family. Keep the bond alive by hiring an adult babysitter (maybe once per week) and having a date night only you and your partner.

Let things flow a bit. I'm not always great at this however it's something I try to improve on regularly Do not be always so rigid. Let things flow. It's a child's play. Let them be kids. I'm extremely strict when it comes to things However, I always remind myself of the fact that this isn't worth the stress of trying to make their case about certain things. Instead, let things slide and relax. You'll be perfect in the end in the long run, as that you are in love with them them and help the people you love and support them.

Decluttering can be a family-friendly event. I prefer to schedule an occasion every couple of months to look through all the things in our homes and get rid of it. We do it as a group, and it's an opportunity to bond. We leave with trash bags full of rubbish boxes full of things to give away or donate to our family members and at the end, much less cluttered rooms. It's extremely satisfying.

Relax at your home. We are often too busy to be traveling every minute of the day, traveling to one place or another. If we're having time with the family, it's typically spent in the car too and going to the movies , restaurants or any other events that are fun.

However, it can be exhausting and costly. Instead, you should try spending your time at home as frequently possible. You can enjoy the DVD instead of heading to the cinema and enjoy popcorn. You can play games on the board or play outside in the sun and engage in a game. You can read to one another or in solitude or even tell stories. There are plenty of activities you can perform at home, for nothingand are enjoyable and relaxing.

Make traditions. Kids are fond of holidays, from Christmas traditions to family customs. My mom loves all of our children to visit prior to Christmas time to bake Christmas cookies, or to come in before Easter to decorate eggs. Kids love these rituals. It is also possible to create rituals at home regardless of whether it's the time for a family meal or family Meetings as well as Family Day, or anything that brings people together. If you establish it as a routine event, and you give it extra significance, it'll become an ongoing tradition and will be something your children keep in mind throughout their lives.

Create cooking and cleaning as an activity for the whole family. Cleaning and cooking are complex tasks, and they can drain your time from your children. Engaging in these activities as a family can solve both issues - getting everyone involved helps to make cooking and cleaning easier as well as give you quality time with each other while teaching your children important life abilities. Have fun with it by letting them choose recipes, and then shop for the ingredients with you. Find out how fast you can get the house cleaned up. home -- if all of my family members participate and helps, it can be done in 30 to 40 minutes. Make it an activity or task.

Reduce commitments. This is applicable to the commitments you make and your children' commitments. If you are overwhelmed by commitments things to do, your life is difficult. If you can reduce the commitments the life of your reduced. It's as simple as that. Create a list of all your family's obligations and then determine what ones are in line with your goals as well as which are most crucial.

Which ones bring you most enjoyment and satisfaction? What ones take up your energy and time and do not give much in exchange?

Maintain the main commitmentsboth yours and those of your children -- and get rid of as many other obligations as you can.

Be active. Nowadays, children can be very uninvolved (and unhealthy) because of all the television, Internet, and video games they play. Keep them active by taking them outdoors with them, taking strolls, taking a swim and playing games. My family enjoys playing football or soccer. You can play freeze-tag. If you're running the kids with you at least for a part or all the way. Take them on bikes and take them for a ride in the parks. Make them do challenges, such as races, pushups as well as pullup challenge. Keep it fun, but make sure they are active. What can this do to make your life easier? It means that they use less media I believe this can be a problem. It also ensures their health at a low cost and reduces your healthcare expenses later on.

Be focused on what you do rather than spending. We often send messages to our children on how to live their lives according to the things we do. We love to shop eating out, or go to the theater Our children discover that having fun is spending money. We tend to focus on the material and, consequently, do our children. Instead, show your children (by talking , but also through how you act) that the key is doing things and not spending money on things. Walk around at the parks, enjoy playing outdoors and play board games, tell stories, read or play charades, cook and clean up, go to the lake or beach as well as build something and clean the car. Spend quality time with friends engaging in activities that don't cost you anything.

Things You can Do in the lead-up to the Moving Day

In the months, weeks and days that lead up to your move, you can try these exercises to make it easier to your kid.

• Break the News According to the U.S. Census Bureau, one in six Americans relocates each year. Parents must inform their children about the move every day and now is your turn. Be patient until you have your child's full attention, and then, calmly and with a clear mind, clarify what's going on. Be aware that this is a significant change and that many things will change, but be sure that your child is aware how the unit of your family and the traditions are not going to change.

Create a Book Instruct your child to write an account of your childhood home. Based on your child's age and stage, you might be required to help to a certain extent. Include photos along with descriptions of the old house. Family members can talk about their best images of their home as well. This will create an item that your child will cherish.

Visit the new Home and Neighborhood if feasible, bring your child to see the new house whenever you are able. Explore the neighborhood to discover important landmarks such as schools, parks supermarkets, grocery stores, and cinemas.

* Take pleasure in moving-themed books and Movies - Visit the library to get films and books that are themed to moving. The best options for both are readily available since moving is a huge and significant part of the lives of children. After reading an article or watching a movie with your child and discuss what the characters did to cope through the experience.

Let Your Child Take Certain Decisions as a parent it's normal to feel the need to take over the reigns in planning an upcoming move. But, if children feel helpless and insecure, they're more likely to be anxious and worried about the upcoming move. Make sure to involve children in the process of making decisions when it makes sense. As an example allow them to choose the room they want to use, and then solicit their opinions on what items to keep and which items should be donated, sold or to be disposed of.

* Save Some Older Items - One major advantage of moving is that you are capable of getting rid of useless stuff. But don't do it in the way that is detrimental to your child's safety, but. Try to allow your child to hold some items, and to keep one or two antique pieces of furniture so that the brand new home appear more familiar.

Go to at the New School - As early as you can, take your children to their new school they will be attending. Register them as soon as you can to avoid any confusion in the beginning. If you can, visit the new school to ensure your child is able to understand the general idea of what's happening. You can make it easier by going to the school prior to their first day to ensure that they will be able to meet their teacher or teachers and the principal. It is possible to request to have a friend for your student to play with during your first day.

* Let the Movers do the work - It's much easier to be present with your kid when you're not performing all the lifting. Find a moving company to let professionals do the heavy lifting while you concentrate on the logistics, and keep your child engaged and entertained all day long.

* Hire a Sitter If your child isn't old enough to help find a sitter, ask for one. A responsible adult to watch your child's progress will make their day less stress-inducing.

moving-children-suitcase* Put Together a Moving Day Bag - Avoid the stress of hunting high and low for a specific item for your child by helping them pack a special moving day bag. Make sure to start for at the very least one week in advance to make sure that everything they require is contained. Make sure to pack it with their most loved toys, books electronic gadgets, and other things they have come to know. Make sure to have a change of clothes , a pillow or blanket that your kid can use when arrival at the new location.

• Play New House Hide and Seek When you arrive at your new home Take some time from unpacking to have a fun game with your children. This is an excellent method to let your child get acquainted with their new house and also keep them entertained.

* Let Your Child Take things away - You might have your own ideas about the location and the way things will be laid out at the new location However, you must involve your child's input in the process as well. This will allow your child to become the owner of their new residence and to feel as if they have some influence over what's happening and makes the whole process more manageable.

* Go camping Indoors in the New Place - The first night spent in a completely unfamiliar location can be a bit scary. Change it into an adventure by letting your child make camp inside that first night. Bring a tent to the home, then let them set the tent in the way they want. Share "campfire stories" and engage in other camp-related activities to keep your child happy and engaged.

* Keep a Moving Day Journal Offer older children blank journals they can keep a record of the transition to a new place. The day of the move they can use it to be able to express their thoughts on everything that's happening. Then, they can take pleasure in reviewing their initial impressions of their new home.

Have Fun with Old packing materials - As excited as you are to throw away your old packing supplies, put them off for a few days. Play with your child the boxes from years ago as well as packing peanuts and other things. Forts and other constructions can distract them from all the obstacles of everyday life.

Set up Your Child's Room Prior to that, make the placement of your child's bedroom the first priority. When their room is set up according to their preferences and is organized, they will be able to have their own space packed with items they are familiar with that they can retreat to whenever the necessity arises.

* Meet your neighbors - Don't wait around for your neighbors to greet you. Instead, take an outing together with your kid and then introduce yourself. There are at the very least a few youngsters your child's age walking in the streets which is the best method to locate them.

* Go to your Old Neighborhood - Schedule trips to the old neighborhood following the day of moving. Your child will be looking eagerly to visit their old street and their friends for the first time, and it helps help ease the transition.

* Keep in Touch Inspire your child to keep connected to acquaintances from their previous city. If they're older enough to be able, using social media could assist in this manner. If they're younger remain in touch with their parents' friends and sometimes arrange for the kids to connect via the phone or through an app for video.

Let Your Child Express their feelings - Moving can be stressful for both of you You may be tempted to appear as if everything is okay and expect other people to behave similarly. Your child must be able to process the entire situation and discuss it with their parents and other family members is the best method to do this. Ask your child regularly what they think about the change to ensure they are expressing their emotions effectively.

Anyone with kids understands that any family life is bound to be a bit complicated at the very least to a certain extent. From laundry and bathing and cooking , shopping and school and driving and sports and crisis and dance , toys and tantrums There's no shortage of issues.

It's not possible to live a life that is super-simple life if you have youngsters ... however, you can figure out ways to simplify your life, regardless of how many children you have.

Take my personal life as an instance, I'm the proud owner of children in my home Yet I've managed to find ways to simplify my life and find peace and joy in the chaos. What is the method by which this trick can be achieved? It's nothing magical, in fact only a few small things that have made my life simpler throughout the many years.

The most important trick however, is making my family my main priority and making one or two priorities within my daily life. If you're overwhelmed with things you'd like to do or have to complete and you're living a life that's complex. If you pick just certain things that matter for you, then you will be able to cut out the rest, and make your life much simpler.

This list that could be confusing to some people -- 25 items! Believe me, I could easily expand this list, however I'm not trying to overload you with too many options. Do not try to address all the items on this list at one time Pick a few ideas you are interested in, and try them. Keep this list in mind and refer back to periodically to explore other options. The best part is that they could give you ideas for your own!

Self-sufficiency. This tip could simplify your life in the long run. But, it could create more complications in the short-term. The goal is to train your children to take on tasks independently as they grow older and more skilled. Learning to complete tasks by themselves rather than doing it by themselves takes time and may be quite difficult initially, but eventually this will come back in the end if you keep going.

Conclusion

When dealing with children, parents and teachers often have difficulty getting children to understand and to follow the instructions. It's a huge achievement to be a defender for children and help them stay on the right path. When you have to be in contact with a youngster, it can be difficult to communicate, comprehend and hear to develop the ability to help the child. If all of these aspects are in place, then it could create a harmonious relationship with your child until maturation. If parents and teachers are looking to establish an open and stable environment, they should use this amazing book. It will help you develop communication skills and assist in your interactions with children.

www.ingramcontent.com/pod-product-compliance
Lightning Source LLC
Chambersburg PA
CBHW050402120526
44590CB00015B/1786